The Aegean World

Translated by Ewald Osers

Alfred Nawrath

The Aegean World

Peloponnese Sporades Cyprus

With 93 colour illustrations

Joseph J. Binns · Publisher · Washington–New York

Colour photographs Alfred Nawrath †, Bremen

Graphical presentation Kümmerly & Frey, Geographical Publishers, Berne

Cartography, photolithography and offset-printing

Kümmerly & Frey, Geographical Publishers, Berne

© 1969 Kümmerly & Frey, Geographical Publishers, Berne/Switzerland

Printed in Switzerland

Published in the United States 1978

ISBN 0-88331-097-X

Library of Congress Card Catalog Number 77-088796

Translator's Note

The spelling of Greek names in English is totally inconsistent—not only between one author and another, but frequently within the same book or atlas. Names of places and persons associated with ancient Greece and classical Greek literature are traditionally rendered in their latinized forms (Halicarnassus, Hephaestus); a few others (Athens, Corinth, Salonica, Cephalonia) have time-honoured anglicized forms. A great many more are found in transliterations which are not even consistent within themselves (Calymnos). Finally, there is the uncertainty whether transliteration should be based on the classical or the modern form of the language (Hagios-Ayios). An attempt has been made by the translator to render all names in the form in which they are most commonly found in reputable works of reference or on the maps most likely to be consulted. The continuous use of alternative forms in brackets, when only one or two letters are affected (Ithaca—Ithaka, Leucos—Levkos—Lefkos, Cythera—Kithera), would have been an irritating and unnecessary exercise in pedantry.

Contents

Mediterranean Archipelago

ALFRED NAWRATH

The Ionian Islands 13
The Peloponnese 14
Crete 16
Thessaly 17
Epirus 18
Mount Athos 19

Chaeroneia and Marathon... 20
Cyclades 20
The Dodecanese 23
Western Asia Minor 24
Cyprus 31

Greece

JEAN M. PANAYOTOPOULOS

Journey through Hellas 33
The Immortal Legend 41

Historical Destiny 46
Greece and the Sea 52

Aegean Asia Minor

CEVAT SAKIR

The Hellespont 57
Anatolia 60
Assos 64
Pergamum 66
Izmir 70
Ionia 73

Ephesus 78
Halicarnassus 85
Hierapolis 90
Lycia 92
Pamphylia 94

Cyprus

WALTER STAEHELIN

Island of Many Facets 99
Legend 99
Byzantium and the National
Church 100
The Princes of Lusignan 103
Venetian Intermezzo 105

Turkish Rule 105
Britain's Key to the East 107
The 1959 Treaties 108
Outbreak of the Conflict 109
Greeks and Turks 111
The Economy 115

Plates

Ionian Islands

1 Corfu. The monastery island of Vlacherna and Pontikonisi
2 Assos. On the west coast of Cephalonia
3 Ithaca. View from above the fountain of Arethusa
4 Marathia. On the southern tip of Ithaca

Peloponnese

5 Bassae. Temple of Apollo Epicurius
6 Marathonisi. On the Gulf of Laconia
7 Olympia. Temple of Hera and Hill of Cronus
8 Messene. Ancient city walls, now buried and over-grown
9 Mistra. Monastery of Pantanassa and Frankish fortress
10 Old Corinth. Temple of Apollo
11 Arcadia. Near Sparta
12 Karytaena. Frankish castle of the thirteenth century
13 Gulf of Corinth. Rising storm
27/28 Patras. Greek cheese and wine
64 Pyrgos. Glyphada caves

Crete

14 Harbour of Khania
16 Herakleion. Grain harvest
17 Storage jar at the Vronisi Monastery
18 Palace of Minos in Cnossus
19 Windmill in the Lassithi valley
39 Zakros. Peasant woman threshing grain

Thessaly

20 Delphi. Between the Temple of Apollo and the Castalian spring
21 Preveza. Springtime on the Ambracian Gulf
22 Konitza. Ancient Turkish bridge
23 Meteora rocks north of Kalabaka
24 Kastraki. 'Castle of the Holy Grail', Meteora mountains

Epirus

25 Arta. Apse of the Church of St. Basil
26 Kastoria. Old Turkish farmhouse with oriel window

Mount Athos

29 Monastery of Simopetra
30 The Great Lavra. Refectory and well-house
31 Russian monk and Panteleimon Monastery
32 Dionysos Monastery

Boeotia

33 Chaeroneia. Memorial of the battle fought in 338 B.C.
34 Marathon. The battlefield of 490 B.C.

Cyclades

35 Hydra. Between the Saronian Sea and the Gulf of Argolis
36 Old Athens. View from the Acropolis towards Mount Lycabettus
15/37 Thera.
38 Thera. Ancient crater wall dropping steeply into the sea
40/87 Chios.
41 Delos. One of the five archaic lions
42 Naxos. Marble quarry
43 Naxos. Unfinished statue near Apollona
44 Paros. Ancient columnar drums used in medieval fortress walls
45 Naxos. Rough-hewn statue
46 Paros. Bells among the branches of a tree
47 Paros. Fishing port of Naussa
48 Amorgos. Panayia Choroviotissa Monastery
49 Ios. Harbour and church
50 Ios. Upper town
51 Ios. Chapels and terraced vineyards
52 Ios. Street with passageway

Dodecanese

53 Patmos. Byzantine chapel
54 Patmos. Harbour of Scala, seen from the monastery
55 Patmos. Cave of St. John the Divine
56 Patmos. Bells of Ayia Anna
57 Patmos. Upper town and fortified monastery
58 Rhodes. Rock terrace with Temple of Athena Lindia
59 Rhodes. Lindos with temple fortress
60 Rhodes. Castle of the Knights of St. John and Turkish clock-tower
61 Rhodes. Mosque of Suleiman the Great with minaret
62 Castelorizo. View from an olive grove
63 Castelorizo. Dawn over islands and sea
65 Cos. Abandoned rock dwellings

Western Asia Minor

66 Assos. Troad coast facing Lesbos
67 Pergamum. Theatre on the acropolis
68 Izmir. Old Smyrna with agora
69 Priene. Alluvial plain of the Maeander
70 Ephesus. Basilica of St. John and citadel
71 Halicarnassus. Castle of the Knights of St. John

72 Pamukkale. Limestone sinter terraces of Hierapolis
73 Gulf of Kerme. Under the Turkish flag
74 Xanthos. Necropolis of the Lycian capital
75 Soeke. Young women in native Turkish dress
76 Anatolia. School and mosque
77 Anatolia. Artesian well in the steppe
78 Belkis. Old Seljuk bridge
79 Manavgat. Last rapids before the sea
80 Alanya. Harbour, jetty and Red Tower
81 Antalya. Mosque of Ala ud-Din Kaikobad
82 Anamur Kalesi. Corsair fortress facing Cyprus
83 Side. Theatre of the Fourteen Thousand
84 Myra. Ancient Lycian rock tombs with dressed-stone façades
85 Turkish Riviera. Between Antalya and Mersina

Cyprus

86 Premonstratensian abbey near Kyrenia
88 Early Christian icons at Lambusa
89 St. Nicholas Cathedral, Famagusta
90 Byzantine church near Lambusa
91 Paphos, on the western coast
92 Mosaics of Curium near Episkopi
93 Rock of Aphrodite

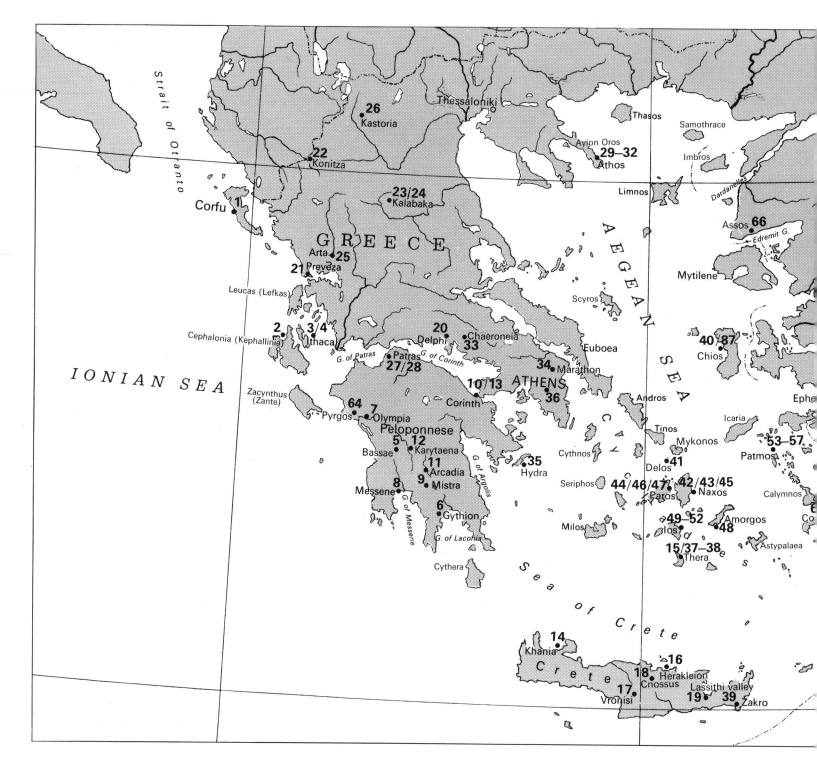

Strait of Otanto

26
Kastoria

Thessaloniki

Thasos

Samothrace

Ayion Oros
29–32
Athos

Imbros

Limnos

Dardanelles

Assos **66**
Edremit G.

22
Konitza

23/24
Kalabaka

Corfu **1**

G R E E C E

Mytilene

Arta **25**

Scyros

21 Preveza

Leucas (Lefkas)

A E G E A N

S E A

Cephalonia (Kephallinia)

2
3/4
Ithaca

20
Delphi • Chaeroneia
33

Euboea

40/87
Chios

G. of Patras
Patras G. of Corinth
27/28

34 Marathon

IONIAN SEA

Zacynthus
(Zante)

10/13 ATHENS

36

Andros

Corinth

Ephe

64 7
Pyrgos • Olympia
Peloponnese

Tinos

Icaria

53–57

Mykonos

Patmos

5 12
Bassae • Karytaena

Cythnos

Delos **41**

Calymnos

11
Arcadia
9 • Mistra

G. of Argolis

35
Hydra

Seriphos

44/46/47
Paros

42/43/45
Naxos

8
Messene

6
Gythion

Milos

49–52
Ios **48**

Amorgos

Co

G. of Messene

Astypalaea

S

15/37–38
Thera

G. of Laconia

Cythera

S e a

o f

C r e t e

14
Khania

16

C r e t e

18
Cnossus

Herakleion

Lassithi valley

17
Vronisi

19 39
Zakro

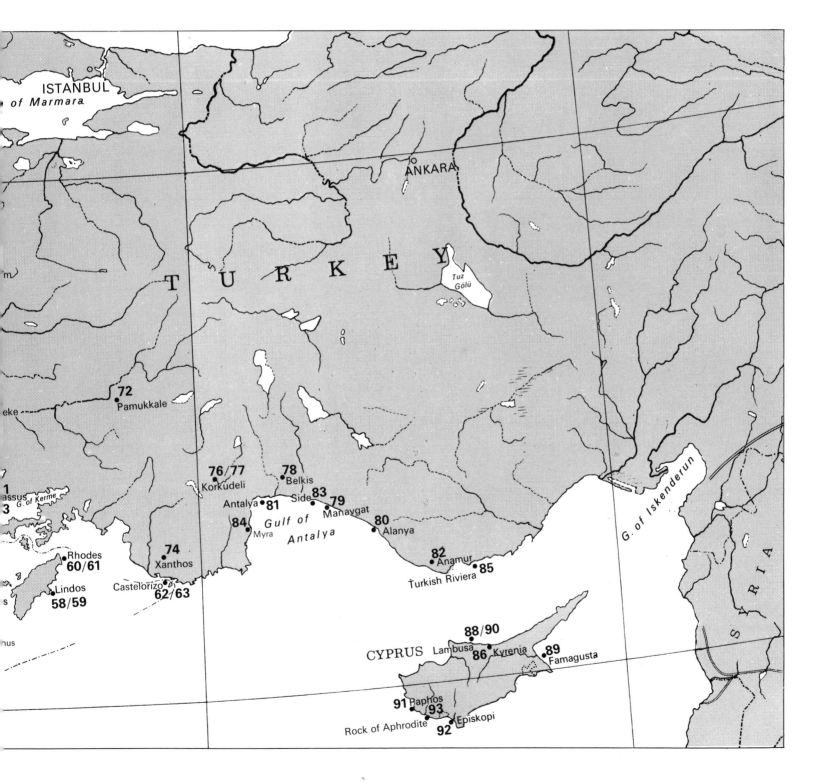

ISTANBUL
of Marmara

ANKARA

T U R K E Y

Tuz
Gölü

72
Pamukkale

eke

76/77
Korkudeli

78
Belkis

83
Side **79**
Antalya **81** Manavgat

80
Alanya

84
Myra

Gulf of
Antalya

82
Anamur

85

Turkish Riviera

1
assus
G. of Kerme
3

Rhodes
60/61

74
Xanthos

Lindos

Castelorizo
62/63

s
58/59

hus

G. of Iskenderun

S
Y
R
I
A

88/90

CYPRUS Lambusa
86 Kyrenia

89
Famagusta

91 Paphos
93
Rock of Aphrodite **92** Episkopi

9

Tell me, O Muse, th' Adventures of the Man,

That having sack'd the sacred Town of Troy,

Wandred so long at sea; what course he ran

By winds and tempests driven from his way:

That saw the Cities and the fashions knew

Of many men, but suffer'd grievous pain

To save his own life and bring home his Crew.

Though for his Crew, all he could do was vain,

They lost themselves by their own insolence,

Feeding, like fools, on the Sun's sacred Kine,

Which did the splendid Deity incense,

To their dire fate. Begin, O Muse divine.

The Greeks from Troy were all returned home,

All that the War and winds had spar'd, except

The discontent Ulysses onely, whom

In hollow Caves the Nymph Calypso kept.

But when the years and days were come about,

Wherein was woven his return by fate

To Ithaca (but neither there without

Great pain), the Gods then pitied his estate.

HOMER's *Odyssey,* I, I-XIX
Translated by Thomas Hobbes of Malmsbury
Third edition, London, 1686

1 CORFU   The monastery island of Vlacherna and Pontikonisi

2 ASSOS On the west coast of Cephalonia

3   ITHACA   View from above the fountain of Arethusa

4 MARATHIA On the southern tip of Ithaca 5 BASSAE Temple of Apollo Epicurius

6   MARATHONISI
On the Gulf of Laconia,
off Gythion

7   OLYMPIA
Temple of Hera and
Hill of Cronus

8 MESSENE
Ancient city walls, now buried
and overgrown

9 MISTRA
Monastery of Pantanassa and
Frankish fortress

11
ARCADIA
Near Sparta

12
KARYTAENA
Frankish castle of
the thirteenth
century

13 GULF OF CORINTH Rising storm

14 WESTERN CRETE Harbour of Khania

17

18

15 THERA
Traditional method
of threshing

16 CENTRAL CRETE
Grain harvest

17 CENTRAL CRETE
Storage jar at the
Vronisi Monastery

18 NORTHERN CRETE
Palace of Minos in
Cnossus

19 EASTERN CRETE
Windmill in the Lassithi
valley   ▷

Mediterranean Archipelago

A mere fifty years ago Greece was like an island in the eastern Mediterranean whose coasts then were Turkish—from the Adriatic coast of Montenegro through Thrace, Macedonia, the Sporades, and Syria, in a sweeping arc all the way to the Tunisian frontier. There were no air or road links then, and between Salonica and the rather sparse rail network of northern Greece there was a gap of some sixty miles. Two Balkan conflicts and two world wars inflicted grievous wounds on the country, but also rescued it from its isolation and gave it the chance of economic advancement. Today, as the tourist flood seems to be turning away from Italy and Majorca, the Aegean world is likely to become an increasingly popular holiday area. Large ferryboats now bring foreign visitors to Greece in a few hours. And like Ulysses they make their landfall at Scheria, the island of the Phaeacians, whose modern name is Corfu.

The Ionian Islands

1 CORFU A springtime panorama, looking towards the small monastery island of Vlacherna which has been linked to Corfu by a causeway ever since antiquity—just like the small island off Gythion (Plate 6). Beyond Vlacherna, rising from the sea, is the island of Pontikonisi with a cypress grove strongly reminiscent of Boecklin's famous painting, *The Island of the Dead*.

2 ASSOS On the west coast of the island of Kephallinia (Cephalonia) the Venetians built a massive fortress to control the approaches to the Gulf of Corinth. The picture, taken from half-way up the ancient fortress, shows the village where Lord Byron, who was particularly fond of the Ionian islands, stayed in 1823:

'The isles of Greece! the isles of Greece! / Where burning Sappho loved and sung, Where grew the arts of war and peace, / Where Delos rose, and Phoebus sprung! Eternal summer gilds them yet, / But all, except their sun, is set.'

Don Juan, Canto III

3 ITHACA   Standing on the rocky bastions in the south-east of Ithaca and looking out over the island-dotted sea one begins to understand the nostalgia which gripped Ulysses at the thought of his home. From the foot of the rock springs the Fountain of Arethusa which has been a symbol of marital fidelity for 3000 years. In Ithaca the words of Homer's epic really seem to come to life. In the darkness of the near-by Grotto of the Nymphs the sorely tried Ulysses, acting upon the advice of his patron goddess Athena, concealed the presents of hospitality he had received from Alcinous. The stone-walled sheep pen of Eumaeus was probably somewhere near Marathia (Plate 4) on the south cape of Ithaca.

The Peloponnese

5 BASSAE   The sturdy Doric columns of the Temple of Bassae and the massive oak in the foreground seem to blend into a harmonious whole. Anyone wishing to explore the secrets of the Greek architect Ictinus will do far better to start his studies at Bassae rather than in Athens at the Parthenon, where the restoration work seems to go on for ever. The temple, built of rough grey limestone, is situated in a remote spot in the mountains, about 3800 feet above sea-level. It was completed in 417 B.C. and gratefully dedicated to Apollo Epicurius.

6 MARATHONISI   The tiny island of Marathonisi, situated just off the port of Gythion on the Gulf of Laconia, was named Cranae in classical antiquity. It was here that Paris found refuge after eloping with Helen and in consequence unleashed a disastrous and protracted war—a war fought, according to Homer and his countless successors, to avenge the abduction of that most beautiful of women, with 'the face that launched a thousand ships, and burnt the topless towers of Ilium' (Christopher Marlowe). On this little island, which is linked to the mainland by a causeway, in the same way as Vlacherna (Plate 1), Phoenician traders offered

their Tyrian purple before the beginnings of recorded history. Later the island and the port of Gythion opposite served the powerful city state of Sparta as a naval base.

7 OLYMPIA This sacred site in Elis is one of the most famous spots on earth. The supreme prize in the games held there was a laurel branch. The athletic contest was invariably linked with an artistic one: it was at Olympia that Herodotus read from his famous History. In later antiquity highly paid professional athletes made their appearance in the stadium; even Roman Emperors competed there in an attempt to win popularity. The games were held every four years at the first full moon after the summer solstice; their discontinuation coincided with the decline of the Roman Empire. Ever since Homer's rhapsodic verses began to conquer the Grecian world in 776 B.C., that world measured time in Olympiads.

8 MESSENE West of Kalamata on the Gulf of Messene lies the ancient site of Messene. The massive wall, once six miles long, which encircled this capital city founded by Epaminondas, is now largely covered in scrub. In its day, however, it excelled all the better-known masterpieces of fortification engineering in Byzantium, on Cyprus, on Gotland, and at Carcassonne.

9 MISTRA Founded in 1240 by Guillaume II de Villehardouin, the ruler of Morea (the Peloponnese), Mistra today is the only site where the development of Greco-Byzantine architecture and painting can be followed continuously over two centuries. On the summit of the hill stands the Frankish castle. Half-way up is the fortified monastery of Pantanassa dating back to 1428; it contains numerous frescoes. The agaves in the foreground were unknown to the ancient Greeks; they were imported from Mexico in the post-Columbian period.

10 OLD CORINTH It was in the year A.D. 50 that the Apostle Paul established the first Christian community on Greek soil—at Corinth, in the shadow of the Temple of Apollo, the foundations of which were laid in the sixth century B.C. Of the twenty-eight original columns only seven remain standing today, some still

carrying their heavy architraves. They are nearly twenty-four feet tall and are a hundred years more recent than the Doric columns of the Temple of Hera at Olympia (Plate 7).

11 ARCADIA NEAR SPARTA   This is how Goethe's Faust saw this landscape in his mind's eye:

'There gush the springs, the brooks leap downwards merging, / Already gorges, slopes, and meads are green; / And far, upon a hundred hills diverging, / The fleecy flocks at pasturage are seen... / And mother-bounty, in the peaceful shadows, / Gives soft the flowing milk for lamb and child; / Fruit is at hand, the mellow fare of meadows, / And hollow trunks drip honey in the wild.'
(GOETHE, *Faust,* Part II, Act III; translated by Philip Wayne (Penguin Books, 1959)

Crete

14 WESTERN CRETE   Like Corfu, Crete today is linked to the Greek mainland by car ferries. Its political union with Greece was achieved in 1913 and was principally the work of Venizelos, the great Greek statesman born near Khania a hundred years ago. A few minarets serve as a reminder of the period of Turkish rule.

16 CENTRAL CRETE   Strung from the middle finger of the hand-shaped Peloponnesian peninsula across to Rhodes in the east, or to the Lycian Section of the Taurus mountain range in Asia Minor, Crete—with a length of 160 miles Greece's largest island—screens off the southern Aegean like a boom, and, in consequence, imparts to it the character of an inland sea. The destinies of Crete were always determined by its geographical situation. Whoever held this island dominated the eastern Mediterranean. Its political capital is Khania, situated on the meridian of Cape Sunium (in Attica); however, most of the traffic to the Greek mainland nowadays goes via Herakleion, in the middle of the north coast, where the island has its greatest width.

16

About 1540 the painter Theotokopuli, who later gained world fame under the name of El Greco, was born in a village west of Herakleion. The fairly recent storage jar at the Vronisi Monastery (Plate 17) shows how little Crete has changed in the course of 3500 years. Similar evidence is provided by the old woman threshing the grain on the eastern coast of Crete (Plate 39). She stands on a threshing sleigh the edges of which curve upwards like runners—a type found already in ancient Babylonian stone reliefs. Contrary to the advice in the Bible that an ass used for threshing should not have his mouth bound up, this peasant woman has muzzled her animals.

18 NORTHERN CRETE Numerous individual finds on view in the Museum of Herakleion combine to provide an integrated picture of Minoan civilization. The enormous storage jars of reddish fired clay excavated at Cnossus (Knossos) were used to store oil, wine, and grain.

19 EASTERN CRETE The idea of Crete as an earthly paradise is instantly exploded by a glance at the soil of the Lassithi plateau which requires elaborate irrigation. The many windmills there are reminiscent of Dutch landscapes before the turn of the century.

Thessaly

20 DELPHI The shades of night have not yet lifted from the last standing columns of the Temple of Apollo. The twilight seems to harbour the shades of all those who, from time immemorial, have come to Delphi from all corners of the earth to listen to the prophecies of the oracle whose advice they solicited and accepted as divine revelation. Below the Phaedriadae rocks runs the spring of Castalia.

21 PREVEZA Only Corot or Van Gogh could have caught the light playing about the marble of the temple columns or the rays of sunlight filtering through the silvery foliage of the olives and weaving the flowers in the grass into a carpet straight out of the Arabian Nights.

23, 24 KALABAKA   Originally there were twenty-three monasteries founded in this wilderness during the turbulent century preceding the conquest of Constantinople by Mohammed II. They stood on vertical pinnacles of rock, frequently accessible only by ladder, or clung to high overhanging rock-faces. Soon the Meteora monasteries will be mere museum pieces as fewer and fewer novices join the order. The conglomerate rocks with their bizarre shapes are objects of special interest to geologists.

Epirus

25 ARTA   Our next picture takes us to ancient Epirus, the mainland region opposite Corfu, the starting point of our visit to Greece. The Ambracian Gulf cuts deep into the mainland, and only a narrow passage links these waters with the Ionian Sea between Corfu, Cephalonia and Ithaca. On the southern shore of the Gulf's mouth lies Actium, where the historic battle between Octavian and Mark Antony was fought in 31 B.C. Arta, the Ambracia of antiquity, is the principal town in the Gulf area and lies on its northern edge not far from the shore. Its Byzantine churches of the thirteenth and fourteenth centuries, the Metropolitan Church of Panayia Parigoritissa and the church of St. Basil, are among the most important of their kind. Greek cultural leanings nowadays are towards Byzantium rather than ancient Greece, especially as the ancient *polis*, the city state, was not a large-scale political organism in a European sense. Only Byzantium gave birth to a great Greek empire. Today Greece is turning back again with enthusiasm to its medieval past: the church of St. Basil (Plate 25) has been beautifully restored.

26 KASTORIA   Near the Albanian-Yugoslav frontier an ancient Turkish farmhouse with oriel windows, one of the few of this type extant, testifies to the artistic effect of a spatial harmony achieved with exceedingly modest means.

27 PATRAS   Whichever of the many Greek cheeses the foreign tourists may prefer, they are almost unanimous in praise of Greek wines, in particular of the dark Mavrodaphne from Patras, which matures not in cellars but under the almost eternally cloudless Greek sky.

Mount Athos

29 SIMOPETRA   In 1963 the monastic republic of Mount Athos celebrated its millenary. The Chalcidice peninsula in the north of the Aegean Sea owes its name to its great mineral wealth and, like the Peloponnese, terminates in three long and narrow peninsulas. The north-eastern tongue of land facing the island of Thasos is taken up by the monks' republic of the Agion Oros, the Holy Mountain. Mount Athos proper reaches a height of 6670 feet; its prominent position in the south-east makes it even more impressive. Ever since remote antiquity it has served as a landmark for mariners. From the timbered galleries of the monastery of Simopetra, 1000 feet above the precipice, there is an incomparable panorama.

30 THE GREAT LAVRA   In 963 the pious monk Athanasius from Trebizond arrived across the Black Sea, roamed through the wild oak forests of the Chalcidice peninsula, and laid the foundations of the Great Lavra monastery. There are two ancient cypresses in the monastery courtyard; one of them could well be a thousand years old.

31 PANTELEIMON   The Russian monk in the picture gazes across the sea to the Panteleimon monastery which has been occupied by Russian monks since the twelfth century. There were 3500 of these monks in the monastery during the final years of the Tsarist empire. Today their number is down to seventy. The Dionysos monastery (Plate 32) was founded in 1385 and is one of the most recent on Mount Athos. Its position suggests one of the monasteries in the Himalayas.

Chaeroneia and Marathon

33 CHAERONEIA A great battle was fought here at Chaeroneia, in Boeotia, in 338 B.C.
The forces of the Athenians were facing King Philip II of Macedonia on the left
flank; the Thebans along the little Cephissus stream were facing the young Alexander
on the right flank. The royal prince, though so far entirely lacking in military experience, annihilated the Theban contingent. Today a stone lion guards the dead warriors
of Thebes. Their memorial bears no inscription since the fortunes of war had not
favoured them. Nevertheless, they did not die in vain. What Greece had been unable
to achieve by its own strength was accomplished by Alexander, to be known as The
Great. The young king, a Macedonian by birth and a Greek by education at the
hands of Aristotle, was instrumental in helping the Grecian spirit to conquer the world.

34 MARATHON The mound of Soros, dominating the plain of Marathon, contains
the bones of the Athenians killed in battle. Athens was lying unprotected as the vast
military power of Darius, King of the Persians, approached. Twenty-six miles was
the distance from Marathon to Athens, the distance which the messenger of victory
covered in his memorable run. Part of the defeated Persian army retreated aboard
their ships; many of them perished in the extensive swamps which then blocked the
way to the north.

Cyclades

35 HYDRA Two thousand years after the Persian onslaught a new enemy arose in
the east, an enemy which threatened not only Greece but the whole of Europe, an
enemy which succeeded in penetrating first to Byzantium, then to Belgrade, and
eventually to the very gates of Vienna. True, Prince Eugene of Savoy averted the
immediate danger, but in 1715 the Peloponnese became part of Turkey. In 1829, after

ten years' fighting, the Greeks achieved their political independence. In this struggle the small island of Hydra, off the Argolis coast, played an important part. At that time it had a population of 40,000 and produced such intrepid men as Konduriottis and Miaoulis. Today its harbour has become quiet, as has also that of Hermoupolis on Syra, now that coastal shipping has given way to high-sea shipping and the near-by port of Piraeus has become an international port.

37 THERA   About half-way between Herakleion on Crete and the island of Naxos lies a large crescent-shaped island, its sickle facing towards the west. This is the remaining crater wall of an originally circular volcanic crater; now only two massive fragments are left of it—the island of Apronisi and the larger island of Thera to the north of it. The region continues to be active to this day, as witnessed by the volcanic eruptions of 1925 and 1928 and by the earthquake of 1956. In ancient mythology the island was known as Kalliste, 'the most beautiful', and attracted settlers even in pre-Homeric times. Since no trees grow on the volcanic soil, the inhabitants live in caves which they cut out of the volcanic tufa and pumice-stone (cf. Plate 65). In Christian times the island was dedicated to St. Irene; its name in the Middle Ages was Santorini or Santorin.

41 DELOS   Of the nine marble lions which originally lined a terrace on the processional avenue along the sacred lake five are still standing. It was here that the swans of Apollo swam, and it was on the shore of this lake that Leto, pursued by a jealous Hera, gave birth to Apollo in the shade of a palm tree. Delos, though barely two and a half square miles in area, was once the heart of the world. French archaeologists have uncovered the secrets hidden under its soil and thus restored the island's past to mankind.

43 NAXOS   Between the harbour of Naxos on the western coast of the island of the same name and the town of Apollona lie twenty-five miles of paradisiac landscape. It was on Naxos that Dionysus celebrated his marriage to Ariadne after she had been abducted from Crete by Theseus and abandoned there.

44 PAROS   Since the Greek mailboats call only infrequently at these islands we are ferried across to Paros by a fishing-boat. Paros is separated from Naxos by a narrow sound. Our first visit is to the ancient quarries where the white marble used to be cut underground by torchlight; that is why it was known as *lychnites*. Paros was the birthplace of Agoracritus, the brilliant disciple of Phidias, and of the great Scopas, the son of the sculptor Aristander. It was Scopas who created the famous frieze of Amazons on the Mausoleum of Halicarnassus. The Hermes of Praxiteles is chiselled from translucent Parian marble. This marble was also used for the drums making up the columns of the Temple of Hera; these columnar drums were used later in the foundation walls of a medieval fort. One of the most valuable ancient chronicles extant is likewise engraved in Parian marble, revealing the history of mankind over 1318 years—from the age of Cecrops, the legendary King of Athens, down to the year 253 B.C. Not far from the spot where a slab of this Parian marble is preserved today, a strange cluster of small bells hangs suspended among the branches of a tree (Plate 46). The Greeks are fond of hanging bells in the protective shade of an old tree: we find the practice at the Megaspilaeon monastery in the Peloponnese, and at Arta in northern Greece (Plate 25), where the bells hang among the branches of a cypress.

48 AMORGOS   A steep stony footpath leads up from Chora on the island of Amorgos to the Panayia Choroviotissa sanctuary. Two monks are now the only occupants of this spacious monastery which clings to the rock-face and is built back into a natural cave. It was founded in 1088.

49 IOS   This island north of Thera, forming an equilateral triangle with Amorgos and Naxos, is said to be the place where Homer lies buried and where his mother Klimene was born. The terraced slopes, dotted with occasional shrines, are covered with vines. The narrow streets with their vaulted passageways provide shade in the summer.

The Dodecanese

53 PATMOS After leaving the Cyclades, which are grouped in a circle around the sacred island of Delos, we make for Patmos, halfway between Delos and the coast of Asia Minor. Patmos is barren and in antiquity did not attract many settlers. Such early inhabitants as there were venerated Artemis, who was believed to have been born on Delos like her brother Apollo. Her altar stood on the spot where in 1088 St. Christodulos, a native of Bithynia, built a fortified monastery (Plate 57). That was in the same year as the building of the monastery of Amorgos. Both these monasteries have the character of fortresses and were impregnable to the weapons of the day. Plate 54 shows the view from Chora, the main town below the monastery, down to the harbour of Scala. Between it and the upper town lies a cave, now developed into a chapel, where, according to tradition, St. John the Divine lived and where he made his disciple Prochoros write down the Apocalypse. No visitor to Patmos who has ever looked out from the window of the monastery library, who has viewed the Emperor Alexius Comnenus's deed of dedication with the great seal of Byzantium, or who has read some pages of the manuscript Gospel according to St. Mark, with its gold lettering on purple parchment, can ever forget this island.

58 RHODES Situated on a prominent peninsula south of the principal city of Rhodes, in the middle of the eastern coast, is Lindos with its temple and sacred precinct of Athena Lindia, dating back to the fourth century. Only a few sacred sites of the ancient world compare with this Temple of Athena in its breathtakingly beautiful position. The Acropolis of Athens is a long way from the sea; in Lindos, on the other hand, settlement, sea and temple fortress (Plate 59) form an inseparable whole. Already Pindar in his seventh Olympian ode praised Rhodes and the Heraclidae. Engraved in letters of gold in marble, this hymn adorned the Temple of Athena Lindia which was completed about the middle of the fourth century B.C. One thousand nine hundred years later Suleiman the Magnificent entered Rhodes after

a siege of sixteen months. The Knights of St. John sought and found refuge in Malta. The Turkish Sultan was a native of Trebizond; he was a son of Selim I, the first caliph of the Osman dynasty, and it was he who brought the Osman empire to the peak of its glory. In 1529 he began the siege of Vienna. The large court of this emperor included Minar Sinan, perhaps the greatest architect of all time, who built numerous mosques and palaces. The mosque of Suleiman the Great in Rhodes (Plate 61) was built by Sinan shortly after the capture of the island.

62, 63 CASTELORIZO (KASTELLORIZZO)   Castelorizo is reached from Rhodes in a few hours by a small Greek coastal steamer. It forms the most southerly point of Greece and belongs to the group of the Sporades, extending from Patmos to Rhodes. This group of islands was annexed by Italy in 1912 and renamed the Dodecanese. Castelorizo is only one and a half nautical miles away from the small Turkish port of Kas, and contains numerous reminders of its Osman past. Castelorizo means the red fortress and was so named, because of the red colour of the island's rock, by a Grand Master of the Order of St. John at the end of the fourteenth century. It contains a Blue Grotto, inaccessible when the sea is rough; both in size and in its splendid colour it far surpasses that of Capri.

Western Asia Minor

TROY   The city of Troy of the sixth excavated layer, with its cyclopean walls, flourished about the middle of the second millennium B.C.; this city was destroyed by an earthquake about 1300 B.C. Troy was situated on the small river Scamander, on a hill which protected it against raids and from where it could guard the Dardanelles. Homer's Trojan War, if stripped of its mythology, was the first struggle for the Straits. It was through the Dardanelles that Jason passed with his Argonauts to bring back the Golden Fleece from distant Colchis. Through this Strait between the

Aegean Sea and the Sea of Marmara passed the early merchant ships which sailed from Miletus and Priene, from Ephesus and Rome, to bring back grain from the shores of the Pontus. Dardanians, Cimmerii and Galatians, Gyges, King of Lydia, Cyrus, King of the Persians, Alexander of Macedonia, Romans, Goths, Byzantines, and Osmans—who can record the names of all the people who passed through this strategic gateway of the ancient world?

66 Assos   We now take a southerly course towards the large Greek island of Lesbos, birthplace of the poet Arion and of Sappho, 'the tenth Muse'. Today a road leads from Ayvacik to Assos; because of its proximity to a prohibited military area, Assos has been accessible to visitors again only since the beginning of 1965. Ancient authors praised Assos as the most beautifully situated Greek city of the old world. Aristotle spent three years at Assos, and it was from there that, according to tradition, the Apostle Paul set out on his journey to the south in A.D. 58.

67 Pergamum   Systematic excavation of ancient Pergamum began in 1878. The frieze of the Altar of Zeus, 394 feet long and 6½ feet high, depicts, in an almost baroque style of representation, the battle of the Gods against the giants—a symbolic glorification of the victory of the Greeks over the barbarians. Eumenes I, succeeded by his son Attalus (who first assumed the title of king), and their descendants set up a library in their capital which contained some 200,000 parchment volumes and was one of the most valuable collections in antiquity. Antony shipped the volumes to Alexandria, as a present for Cleopatra, and there they were lost in the great fire.

68 Izmir   Between Bergama (the modern Turkish name for Pergamum) and Izmir the road approaches the Aegean Sea at Aliaga. There, at Cyme in Aeolia, the Greek poet Hesiod was born about 700 B.C. The picture, taken from the slopes of the Pagos, shows the ancient agora, the market-place, with its colonnades, and in the background the modern port of Smyrna. Beyond the bay lies the place where, both in antiquity and again under Seljuk rule in the eleventh century, the big merchant ships and men-of-war were built. In 1919 Izmir was occupied by Greek troops and a year

later adjudicated to Greece in the Treaty of Sèvres. In 1922 Mustafa Kemal Pasha reconquered the city and more than 100,000 Smyrna Greeks lost their homes.

MILETUS   Homer and Hesiod, Herodotus and Hippocrates, Heraclitus and Pythagoras were all born on the coast of Asia Minor or on the offshore islands. Thales, who first gave us our modern understanding of nature and who flourished in the seventh century B.C., was born in Miletus 200 years before Socrates. Miletus also produced Hippodamus, an inspired town planner, who laid out Priene. A thousand years after him Isidorus, together with his fellow-countryman Anthemius from near-by Tralles, created the Church of Holy Wisdom, or Hagia Sophia, in Constantinople, the capital of the Christian Emperor Constantine—a work of architecture which has gained world-wide fame through its unique dome. The cosmopolitan city of Miletus also produced, in the fifth century B.C., the famous Aspasia, whose beauty and intellect made her one of the most outstanding women of the ancient world and who was the counsellor of Pericles, the great Athenian statesman. The Büyük Menderes, the Great Maeander, a river whose numerous bends have given to our vocabulary the word 'meandering', was once the lifeline of Miletus but is no longer navigable today. In the course of the centuries it has built up a six-mile-wide barrier of alluvial land between the city and the sea, thereby dooming Miletus.

69 PRIENE   This city too was cut off by the alluvium of the Menderes river from the Latmic Gulf, across which the ancient corn ships used to bring grain from the Pontus, the Black Sea. Behind the city, at the Temple of Kore and Demeter, the hill with the fortress rises almost vertically from the plain—a last refuge in times of danger.

70 EPHESUS   The retreat of the sea near Ephesus is due to the Kücük Menderes, the Little Maeander, known in antiquity as the Cayster (Caistros). The Temple of Artemis (or Diana) was one of the Seven Wonders of the World: it reposed upon 127 columns, some of which were decorated with reliefs. The Apostle Paul, who spent three years at Ephesus, preached the Christian faith in this city of Asia Minor. The capital of the Province of Asia, Ephesus flourished again under the Roman emperors

and, as a cultural centre in the eastern Mediterranean, was outshone only by Alexandria. In A.D. 263 the Goths assaulted the gates of the city. In Byzantine times huge monolithic columns and beautifully veined slabs of translucent marble were brought from Ephesus to Constantinople, where many of them were wrecked in 1204 when the city was sacked by the Crusaders. After the Goths, Ephesus suffered from Seljuks, Mongols and Osmans. The Emperor Justinian, who had the Church of Hagia Sophia in Constantinople built by Anthemius of Tralles and Isidorus of Miletus, also had the church in Ephesus built which contains the tomb of St. John the Divine. Next to the Hagia Sophia and the Church of Apostles in Constantinople, this was the largest church in the Byzantine world and in 1330 was converted into a mosque by the Seljuks. Across the marble columns of the Basilica of St. John we have a fine view of the citadel with its crenellations and fortified towers. The citadel, too, dates back to the Byzantine period and was subsequently enlarged by the Seljuks.

71 HALICARNASSUS   A narrow strait separates Cos from Halicarnassus, and only a quarter of a century separates Hippocrates and Herodotus, who was known even to the ancients as 'the father of history'. Like Aeschylus, with his pronounced faith in eternal justice, Herodotus too saw the decline of the Persian Empire as a divine punishment sent down on its king. The city of Bodrum was at one time subject to King Croesus of Lydia but was later ruled by the Carian dynasty of the Lygdamides who had been put on the throne by the Persians. Artemisia the Elder, a daughter of Lygdamis, took part in the battle of Salamis on the Persian side, contributing five ships to the fleet. The British Museum in London has a colossal statue of the Carian King Mausolus, who, together with his sister-consort Artemisia II, ruled over Halicarnassus from 377 to 353 B.C.; Halicarnassus was then the capital of the whole of Caria. The Mausoleum, the enormous tomb which was built for the King, was one of the Seven Wonders of the World and has since enriched the international vocabulary as a term for a princely tomb of impressive scale. In 1522, when the Osmans were closing in on the city, the last walls of the Mausoleum were dismantled and the large

stone blocks built into the fortress of St. Peter. On the island of Zephyria, where this fortress, known in Turkish as Bodrum Kalesi, stands to this day, once stood the splendid marble palace of King Mausolus.

72 PAMUKKALE   After a few hours' journey in an eastern direction we come to Denizli, reached by the railway which continues to Antalya and Konya. North of it lie the massive ruins of ancient Laodicea, today an abandoned site. At Pamukkale are the even more impressive monuments of ancient Hierapolis. The flat sinter-pans, arranged in descending terraces, whose over-spilling waters have become petrified into strange cascades in the course of thousands of years, are among the most curious natural phenomena on earth.

73 THE GULF OF KERME   The distances separating Assos from Lesbos, Cesme from Chios, Kusadasi from Samos, Bodrum from Cos, are quite slight—but the political distance which has been dividing Greeks and Turks ever since the Cyprus conflict, and hence the political distance between the Turkish mainland and the off-shore Greek islands, has grown immeasurably.

Hippocrates, the greatest physician of the ancient world, the man who raised medicine to the status of a science and who made his disciples swear an oath of professional ethics valid to this day, was born on the island of Cos about 460 B.C.

74 XANTHOS   After our visit to the Troad and to ancient Lydia and Caria we now leave the Aegean coast of Anatolia and turn towards Lycia, the projecting south-western coast of Turkey. The ancient capital of Lycia was the town of Xanthos, situated on a river of the same name. Its necropolis contains turret-shaped monuments and tombs in the shape of small houses. These free-standing monuments date back to the sixth to fifth pre-Christian centuries and show Ionian forms, although they were probably made by non-Greeks.

75 SOEKE   Young women in Turkish native dress filling their finely shaped burnt-clay water jugs near Soeke, not far from Priene and the wine-growing island of Samos, which is separated from the mainland by a narrow strip of water.

21 PREVEZA Springtime on the Ambracian Gulf

22   KONITZA   Ancient Turkish bridge

23 THESSALY Meteora rocks north of Kalabaka

24 KASTRAKI 'Castle of the Holy Grail', Meteora mountains

25
ARTA
Apse
of the Church
of St. Basil

26
KASTORIA
Old Turkish
farmhouse
with oriel
window

76 IN ANATOLIA   A village on the way from the sinter-terraces of Pamukkale to Antalya on the southern coast. Some 3700 miles of Turkish frontier are washed by the sea, not counting the Sea of Marmara which lies within Turkey's frontiers. The mountain ranges of the Pontus in the north and the Taurus in the south form the natural bastions of the country, but unfortunately they also keep the rain-clouds away from the interior, which, in consequence, consists of treeless steppe-land with numerous undrained salt-lakes. The narrow cultivable strip of land between the Black Sea and the Pontus mountains is rich, above all, in hazelnuts; the north coast also supplies tobacco, rice and tea, but cannot, of course, equal the south coast either in scenic beauty or fertility. Between 1930 and 1960 the population of Turkey doubled, and today numbers 31,000,000. In order to reclaim the land and provide employment for the people, the steppe must be pushed back farther and farther—and, with the desert, the camels will soon disappear from the Turkish landscape.

78 BELKIS   In ancient times the turbulent Eurymedon river was navigable as far as Aspendos near Belkis. This was then an enormously wealthy trading centre with a theatre—wellpreserved to this day—capable of holding 20,000 spectators. Twenty-five miles south-east of Aspendos flows the *Manavgat* (Plate 79). Even after several days' continuous rain its waters are emerald green and crystal clear. The stream rises in the Seytan group of the Taurus; it owes its plentiful waters to subterranean tributaries.

80 ALANYA   Along the road to the east, situated by the sea, lies ancient Coracesium, present-day Alanya. Its task was to guard Cilicia and the so-called Cilician Gate, the passage into Syria, Persia, and Mesopotamia, against the threat from Pamphylia. This was the route taken by the powerful Persian kings and by Alexander the Great. Today it has lost its importance since the railway-line from Istanbul to Baghdad passes through the Taurus tunnel.

81 ANTALYA   Piracy along the south coast of Anatolia is as old as recorded history. Pompey had to take action against the pirates as did, 1300 years later, the Seljuk ruler

Ala ud-Din Kaikobad, who frequently resided at Coracesium. In 1225 he had built an octagonal tower of large red stone blocks on the very edge of the sea; this tower is still known as Kizil Kule, the Red Tower. It protected the harbour and the shipyard where ships have been built for 700 years. Antalya can thus boast of having the oldest shipbuilding yards in the world. The timber for the ships came from the majestic cedars of the Taurus. Ala ud-Din Kaikobad also impressed his stamp on Antalya by converting the existing Byzantine church into a mosque. The tall minaret of this mosque, built to the greater glory of Allah, is among the most beautiful of its kind. From its gallery there is a splendid view across the city of Attalus I, King of Pergamum, and Ala ud-Din Kaikobad, guarded in the east by the Ak-Dag mountain in the Cilician Taurus and in the west by the Lycian Taurus.

82 ANAMUR   Corsairs recognized the strategically important position of the city of Anamur, ancient Anemourium. At the spot where Asia Minor reaches out farthest to the south and comes closest to the island of Cyprus they built Anamur Kalesi, a foreshore castle with thirty-six square and round towers which rendered it virtually impregnable.

83 SIDE   This site is half-way between Alanya and Antalya; an Arabian geographer of the twelfth century called it Eski Antalya, meaning ancient Antalya. The city was evacuated by its inhabitants between the seventh and ninth centuries as the sea was increasingly washing up various deposits on the coast.

85 THE TURKISH RIVIERA   About 150 B.C. Attalus II founded the city of Antalya, calling it Attaleia after himself and making it the capital of Pamphylia, the region to the east of Lycia. At Antalya the Cilician Taurus forms a wide arc reaching well out to the south, as far as Tarsus, the birthplace of the Apostle Paul. This fertile strip of land, protected by the Taurus from the cold northerly winds, is known to geographers as the Turkish Riviera. Here olives grow, as well as oranges, lemons, peaches, apricots, almonds and figs—a mere two hours by road from the rocky Anatolian steppe, some 3000 feet above sea-level, where drinking water is at a premium.

Cyprus

The first mission journey of St.Paul the Apostle was from A.D. 45 to 49. When he made his landfall at Antalya he was accompanied by Mark and Barnabas. The latter was born in Cyprus, the son of a Jewish-Levitical family, and it was there that he died a martyr's death in A.D. 75.

86 KYRENIA Premonstratensian monks, who had established a community near Laon in 1120, were called to Cyprus by the royal house of Lusignan, where they built a monastery in the French Gothic style near Kyrenia on the north coast. They called it Abbaye de la Paix, a name which has become Bellapaïs. The church, the refectory, the dormitory and a cloister with an ancient Roman sarcophagus are well preserved to this day.

88 LAMBUSA Ritual lamps and ancient icons, blackened over the centuries by the smoke of candles, reflect the same deep piety as the gilded wood carving above the iconostasis on the island of Chios (Plate 87). Just as temples and columns were symbols of ancient Greece, so the icons symbolize the Byzantine age. From Famagusta (Plate 89) on the east coast of Cyprus it is only a short distance to the Turkish port of Iskenderun, the new Syrian port of Lattakia, or Beirut, the biggest transhipment and free port of the eastern Mediterranean. Famagusta has the most up-to-date port installations in Cyprus. At the same time, its fifty-six-feet-high walls and its elaborates ea fortress with the famous Othello Tower are among the most impressive fortification works of the Middle Ages. The Cathedral of St.Nicholas was completed by the Lusignan rulers in the fourteenth century. The long tongue of land on the north coast of Cyprus points north-east towards Antakya, which became Turkish again in 1939. At Lambusa (Plate 90), near the present capital of Nicosia, abandoned Byzantine churches and chapels are scattered along the seashore.

91 PAPHOS This city on the western coast of Cyprus was founded, according to tradition, by Agapenor, who was shipwrecked with his companions on his return from

the conquest of Troy. Paphos was the seat of a Roman proconsul, and it was here that the Christian Sergius Paulus governed on behalf of the Emperor Claudius. This made Cyprus the first country to be governed by an adherent of the Christian faith. The foundations of the harbour fortress of Paphos date back to Byzantine times.

92 CURIUM   Near the harbour of Limassol on the south coast of Cyprus rises the Kolossi Castle, the ancient fortress of the Knights of St. John, preserved almost completely intact. To the west of the fortress lies Curium, founded in the seventh century by Greeks from Argos. Its fine coloured mosaics have been left *in situ*.

93 THE ROCK OF APHRODITE   At the spot where this massive rock towers from the sea, eroded by the onslaught of the tides, Aphrodite is supposed by legend to have emerged from the seas—Aphrodite Anadyomene, the spume-born goddess of beauty and eternal youth. This is the story as told by Homer, the blind bard, who has guided our steps from the island of the Phaeacians via Ithaca, Troy and his native Ionian islands, all the way to Cyprus.

Greece

Journey through Hellas

We enter Greece by way of Corfu, the ancient Kerkyra, the northernmost and also the most important of the Ionian islands on what is probably the most attractive approach to Greece. It was on this island, called Scheria by Homer, that the Phaeacian people lived, whose mythical King Alcinous and his daughter, the Princess Nausicaa, so hospitably received Ulysses when he was shipwrecked on the coast and put an end to the hardships of his protracted voyage, the original Odyssey. Together with the other islands of the Ionian archipelago, Kerkyra was under Venetian rule throughout four centuries. In more recent times Corfu played its part in the rise of modern Greece: when the country gained its independence in 1829 the first president of the sovereign state was Kapodistria, a native of Corfu.

The islands of Paxoi, gleaming like silver under the foliage of their olive trees, are separated from the south cape of Corfu by a narrow strait; the channel leading to the largest of these islands is reminiscent of a Scandinavian fiord. Close to the steep coasts of Arcadia is Leucas, where in the sixth century B.C. the Greek poetess Sappho threw herself from a cliff because of unrequited love for the handsome Phaon. Off Paxos, Cephalonia and Ithaca rise from the sea, the latter claiming to be the authentic island of Homer, the birthplace of Ulysses. Nearest to the Peloponnese is Cythera, made famous by the ostentatious rites of the cult of Aphrodite.

The Ionian Sea washes the western coasts of the Peloponnesian peninsula, also called Morea, a mountainous region with numerous plateaux, rivers and architectural remains of all periods of history. If Greece itself is sometimes described as a microcosm, the Peloponnese is in turn a picture in miniature of the Greek world as a whole, embracing its history from antiquity to the present day. The political and strategic importance of the Morea was always considerable. Here was the cradle of Mycenaean culture and dominance until the peninsula came under the rule of the

Spartans. As it was heading for decline, the Morea endeavoured by means of the Achaean League, a military alliance of its principal cities, to resist Macedonian incursions and conquest by the Romans. From 1204 until 1453 the Morea, in the shape of the principality of Mistra, represented the last bastion of declining Hellenism.

The southernmost part of the Peloponnese is taken up by the region of Mani, an arid tongue of land lined by ragged rocky coasts. The amount of cultivable soil there is exceedingly small; the local population lead a hard life and their customs are rough. Ethnically they belong to the Greek race and show certain features of the warlike Spartans, whose methods of education they have also adopted. In one form or another they have also preserved the custom of vendetta, the blood feud springing from injured honour.

Gythion is a picturesque town in the south of Laconia. In its Gulf lies the little island of Cranae where, according to legend, Paris concealed the fair Helen before abducting her to Troy. This part of the Peloponnese is overshadowed by the huge, snow-covered Taygetus mountains which form a fantastic screen, opening here and there into ravines of breathtaking beauty. In the east it dips towards the idyllic valley of the Eurotas, which runs through Sparta. Here Zeus, adopting the shape of a swan, embraced the beautiful Leda, a mortal woman who bore him Helen and the Dioscuri Castor and Polydeuces (Pollux). On a flank of this valley the city of Mistra was built in the Middle Ages; its appearance has remained almost unchanged through the centuries. The walls of its palaces, fortresses and churches testify to a renaissance of Byzantine religious painting just before the fall of the medieval Greek empire.

The fertile region of Messenia west of Laconia extends to the Ionian Sea, by whose coast stood ancient Pylus, the city of Nestor. The systematic excavations currently being conducted there are certain to reveal entirely new archaeological vistas. Off Pylus lies the island of Sphacteria, known since the days of Thucydides, when Cleon captured a Spartan army on the island in 425 B.C. In 1827, during the war of liberation, a decisive naval battle was fought off the island.

34

Messenia is a land of plains and valleys, contrasting markedly with Arcadia in the north, which consists predominantly of mountains and plateaux. The Arcadians, whose speech contains elements of the Doric dialect, are thought to be the descendants of the ancient Dorians. At Tegea in Arcadia some fragments of the Temple of Athena have been preserved, and the charming Vitina is situated in a vast pine forest. On the east coast of the Peloponnese the quaint little town of Malvoisie is perched on a steep pinnacle rising from the sea, linked to the mainland by a narrow road. The medieval houses of this rock settlement are surrounded by a fortified wall. The principal city of Arcadia is Tripolis, situated at the very centre of the Peloponnese on a cool plateau between the Maenalus and the Parnon mountains.

Leaving Arcadia in a north-westerly direction we have on our left the region of Elis, including ancient Olympia, that immortal site, and the Temple of Apollo Epicurius at Bassae; to our right are the regions of Corinth and Argolis. The region of Epidaurus is covered with countless, and often very impressive, ruins. In the well-preserved ancient theatre, amidst a classical landscape, the moving dialogue of the ancient tragedies can still be heard every summer, and the grand passions of the House of Atreus come to life again at the spot over which they ruled. Quite close are the castles of Argos, Tiryns, and Mycenae. Nauplia at the head of the Gulf of Argolis was the capital of Greece before Athens. This charming city is dominated by two fortresses —the Palamidi fortress on its sheer rock, famous under Venetian and Turkish rule, and the Acronaupolis citadel.

The Corinth canal, now spanned by two bridges, divides the Peloponnese from the Greek mainland. Having crossed it we move on via Megara and Eleusis to Athens. The first sight we have of the city, from an elevated point on the road, reveals it nestling by the sea among the mountains Parnes, Pentelicus and Hymettus. In the centre of the city rises the immortal fortified hill of the Acropolis, facing the rocky peak of Mount Lycabettus with the Church of St. George on its summit. The plain around Athens is known as Attica; at its end, on Cape Sunium, stands the Temple of Poseidon. This architectural masterpiece together with the Parthenon on the Acropolis and the Temple of Athena on the island of Aegina off Attica form the three points of what has been called the classical triangle.

Off Cape Sunium in the Aegean Sea lie the islands known as the Cyclades, grouped in a ring around Delos. The most important of these islands are Naxos, Paros, Andros, Kea, Tinos, Santorin, and Syra (Syros); in the south they extend close to Crete. The large island of Crete, half-way between Africa and Europe, was the first place reached in the westward advance of eastern civilization. The whole of this island is traversed by mountain ranges which lend the scenery a strange harsh beauty. Its coasts are picturesque and many of the valleys have great idyllic charm. The archaeological museum of Herakleion as well as the sites of Cnossus and Phaestus contain works of art from the Minoan age which are in no way inferior to those of the classical period.

Like a necklace of precious stones the islands of the Dodecanese, the southern Sporades, are strung out north-east of Crete. Under the scorching sun of the eastern Mediterranean they have become bare and rocky. The most beautiful of them, without any doubt, is Rhodes, beloved of Apollo and Athena; their temples at Lindos have partially survived. Homer lists this city of Lindos among the three great cities—alongside 'white Oloosson' and 'white Kameiros'. The city of Rhodes shows unmistakable traces of Frankish rule: there are massive fortifications, solid-looking towers, and walled castles. Almost as interesting as Rhodes is the strange island of Patmos, where St. John the Divine found refuge in a cave and composed the Book of Revelations. Then there is Calymnos, the island of sponge-fishing, and Cos, where under an enormous plane tree Hippocrates instructed his disciples in the art of medicine in the fifth pre-Christian century and where today stands a shrine to Asclepios (Aesculapius). Another of the Dodecanese islands is Castelorizo, a delightful little island off the south-eastern point of Greece, not far from the Aegean coast of Asia Minor.

36

North of the Dodecanese lie the numerous other islands of the Aegean Sea—Icaria with its hot springs; east of it Samos, sacred to the goddess Hera and the birthplace of Rhoecus and Theodorus, the first artists to practise copper engraving. On Samos, Pythagoras began to study geometry, inspired by Heraclitus' teachings about harmony. The island of Chios is fragrant with the aroma of the trees whose bark yields the delicious resin, mastic. The island of Lesbos, made famous by Alcaeus and Sappho, is a vast olive grove, while Lemnos is the island where Philoctetes was left behind by his shipmates, after having been bitten by a snake on his way to Troy, until Ulysses and Neoptolemus picked him up and brought him along to take part in the siege. To the north-east lies Samothrace, the island where the magnificent Nike was sculpted, that famous Winged Victory which today stands in the Louvre. After a brief visit to the near-by island of Thasos, a jewel in the Aegean Sea, we set course for the northern Sporades. There we make our first landfall on Sciathus, an island famous for its golden sandy beaches.

After Scopelos and Scyros, we reach the large island of Euboea, the Negroponte of the Middle Ages. Its capital, Chalcis, is situated on the narrow canal of Euripos, which separates Euboea from Boeotia and in which, according to legend, Aristotle met his death by drowning. At the time of Hesiod, Chalcis was the capital of the early Grecian world.

We next leave the Aegean islands to set foot on the mainland of Greece. At Thebes we stop near an ancient aqueduct and fancy we can hear the laments of Œdipus who in desperation put out his eyes, or the soft sighs of the gentle Antigone who died with the bloom of youth still upon her. Near the Cithaeron mountains rises Mount Helicon, sacred to the Muses. At the foot of this mountain, in Boeotia, lies a fertile plain, now cultivated throughout its length.

In Boeotia are the cities of Chaeroneia and Orchomenos, where Mithridates was defeated by Sulla in 86 B.C. There, too, is the treasure-house of King Minyas and the shrine of the Charites. In the south-east of Doris and Phocis, not far from Boeotia, rises Mount Parnassus, the legendary abode of the Muses. At its foot lies the splendidly situated Delphi, intersected by deep ravines and crowned by snow-capped peaks. Farther east are Phthiotis and Thessaly, made famous by Leonidas's gallant attempt in 480 B.C. to hold up the armies of King Xerxes of Persia in the pass at Thermopylae with a mere 300 men from Sparta. To the west lies the mountainous region of Eurytania with its chestnut groves and pine forests; Aetolia, by way of contrast, is a region of numerous lakes and lagoons. Its principal city, Mesolongion, earned great glory for itself in more recent days when, during the war of liberation in 1826, its inhabitants made a heroic sortie against the besieging Turkish-Egyptian troops. .

The road leading through Mesolongion starts at Athens. It follows the coast of the Gulf of Aegina past the island of Salamis (where the decisive naval battle was fought against the Persians), crosses the Corinth canal, and follows the Peloponnesian coast to Rhion, where the vehicles are loaded on board a ferry to be carried across the narrow strait. On the far shore the road leads up to Acarnania, past Lakes Lysimachia and Trichonis. On the far bank of the Achelous river, which is crossed by a modern bridge, lies the small fishing town of Amphilochia, the innermost point of the Ambracian Gulf. From there the road winds over a steep mountain range and descends into the fertile plain of Arta. Beyond the historic bridge over the Arachthos, celebrated by the popular Muse, we reach the river Luros and through its impressive gorges approach the plateau of Ioannina at the centre of Epirus, the terminal point of one of the most beautiful itineraries through Greece. The city of Ioannina was the residence of Ali Pasha, the Turkish-Albanian ruler of the Epirus, towards the end of the eighteenth century. His castle, the mosque, the ancient Osman houses and the delightful lake with its mysterious little island lend the city a fascinating, romantic aspect. South of Ioannina, still in the Epirus, is the site of the most ancient oracle in Greece—the Dodona Sanctuary, whose ancient theatre has been restored. In Thesprotia we stand on the banks of the river Acheron and the Acherusian swamp, where,

38

according to ancient belief, Charon awaited the souls of the dead, brought to him by Hermes, to be ferried across to the underworld. South of Thesprotia, near the Ambracian Gulf, stand the ruins of the city of Nicopolis, founded by Augustus to commemorate the victory of his fleet over Antony and Cleopatra. Through the valley of the Kalamas with its many gorges we reach Igumenitza, from where the ferry-boat takes us to Corfu in a couple of hours.

To continue our tour of Greece we return to Ioannina and take the road through the magnificent Katara valley in the direction of northern Thessaly. This part of Greece differs from the rest in many ways. Here, perched on enormous rocky cliffs, are the Byzantine monasteries of the Meteora mountains, where the monks used to be hoisted up in baskets in the old days—although now a stairway has been built to the top. Towards the Aegean Sea, Thessaly is joined in the east by the Magnesia peninsula with Mount Pelion, where numerous varieties of fruit trees flourish and where magnificent beaches, inward-facing along the Gulf of Volos and outward-facing along the Aegean Sea, invite the tourist to linger and swim.

Salonica, at the head of the Gulf of Therma, is capital of Greek Macedonia and second largest city in Greece. It has always been great and powerful, situated as it was on an important Roman and Byzantine military highway, the Via Egnatia, which represented a continuation of the Via Appia (the Appian Way) across the Balkans, down along the coasts of the Bosphorus, all the way to Byzantium. Salonica has become a kind of Byzantine museum, although at the same time it is a modern international metropolis and a gateway to the countries north of the Balkans and indeed to Central Europe.

South of Salonica lies the attractive Chalcidice peninsula with its three promontories of Cassandra, Sithonia, and Athos. The famous monks' republic of Mount Athos is under the supervision of a Greek governor but is independent in its internal administration—rather like an ancient monastery city in Tibet. Athanasius founded the Great Lavra, a dependency of the Patriarchate of Constantinople, in 963. Thanks to generous donations from all parts of the world, the monasteries in the Chalcidice peninsula grew ever more numerous—Dionysios, Stavronikita, Vatopedi, the Serbian Abbey of Chilandari, and the Russian monasteries of Panteleimon and Karakallu were added. Athos is dedicated to the Holy Virgin, but women are denied access.

On the way to Giannitsa we encounter the ruins of Pella, the ancient capital of Macedonia and the birthplace of Philip II and Alexander the Great. Recent excavations here have revealed fascinating mosaics. The main road to eastern Macedonia leads into the region of Serrae, where the Annastenaria celebrations are still held every year in honour of St. Constantine and St. Helen—observances which go back to the ancient pagan festivities in honour of Dionysus. After Serrae we pass the small town of Drama and continue, towards the sea, to the town of Kavalla, laid out like an amphitheatre and today the centre of the tobacco industry. Between these two towns are the ruins of Philippi, the site of the great historic battle in 42 B.C. when Mark Antony and Octavian defeated Brutus and Cassius, Caesar's assassins. Eastern Thrace, with its large cities of Adrianople and Constantinople (Istanbul), is Turkish. The Greek part of Thrace is watered by the rivers Hebrus and Nestus, and crowned by the massive Rhodope range; in the mountains there used to be numerous Byzantine monasteries. In Western Thrace and in the Dodecanese there is a Turkish minority; mosques with minarets in the Muslim style are not infrequent. The most important towns here are Alexandroupolis and Suflion.

From Kastanea, the extreme point of north-eastern Greece, the minarets of Adrianople are visible in the distance. Here the Rhodope link up with the Hemos mountains, beyond which lie extensive plantations of tobacco, grain, and heliotrope. According to legend, Bacchus and his companions set out from the Rhodope mountains after a great feast, and the sacred drunkenness of the god of wine gave birth to Greek comedy and tragedy. This, too, is the landscape where Orpheus with his lyre tamed the wild beasts and where, at a later date, Byzantine hermits devoted their lives to ascetic contemplation and prayer.

40

The Immortal Legend

Greek mythology goes back to the earliest periods of prehistory; later, in the Christian era, it was refashioned, assimilated to Christian beliefs and usages, and later still continued to survive as folklore. In an incomparable multiplicity of forms it reflects the deepest traits of the human character. At times it is based on beliefs common to all nations, at others it is rooted deep in the ancient Eastern religions which developed in the Mediterranean area. But inevitably it betrays its Hellenic origins and the manner in which Greeks have understood and transformed its ideas.

The Mycenaean religion is a very ancient Hellenic set of beliefs reflected, as in so many other civilizations, in a cult centred on ancestor worship and the great mystery of death. The dead were a source of awe, reverence, and piety; they were very rarely cremated. The mortal remains of rulers and dignitaries were buried in magnificent tombs, together with their ornaments, weapons, and articles of daily use. Grave treasure of this kind has been found at Mycenae, which was dominated by the cruel House of Atreus, and at Orchomenos, where the legendary King Minyas ruled the Minyan people who spread in Mycenean times over the north of Boeotia. Simultaneously with the ancestor cult there developed, especially in Crete, the cult of a female deity, of a powerful force symbolizing fertility. In the Cretan sanctuaries we also find the cult of a serpent goddess who assumes various characteristics and bears a number of different names—Dictynna, Britomartis, Aphaea—and who subsequently becomes Artemis (and the Latin goddess Diana), armed with lance and shield, reposing in the shade of an olive tree. Later still her place is taken by Athena, the goddess of wisdom and the arts, venerated in Athens and equated by the Romans with their Minerva.

We know next to nothing of the mythology or traditions of this religion; what little we do know is based on archaeological finds. At the time of Homer and Hesiod these beliefs were being replaced by various more recent cults, but they never entirely disappeared from the imagery and deeper layers of consciousness of the people. Hesiod, the father of the didactic epic, left us a treatise on the origin of the Olympian gods in his *Theogonia*. Homer referred to the same gods, even though his epics, the *Iliad* and *Odyssey,* are concerned with the world of the second pre-Christian millennium. Several hundreds of years after the events he describes, the poet uses the language of his own day and draws on numerous events in the world around him. The Hellenic religion now received its final shape and its mythology became crystallized.

Because of the enormous influence which Homer's epics had on the entire ancient world throughout several centuries, this system of religious beliefs came to be a reflection of classical civilization and an important factor in its spread. As with other Indo-European peoples, the original beliefs of the Greeks were undoubtedly associated with nature. The sun was generally accepted in antiquity as the centre of the universe, and the ancient myths were for the most part attempts to explain natural phenomena. Later the Greeks clothed their observations of the behaviour of heavenly bodies in the shape of legends. Zeus meant the vast bowl of the sky, Poseidon the infinite ocean, Apollo the sun, Artemis the moon, and Hephaestus the fire. Subsequently, the gods came to symbolize human virtues and vices; mythology was transformed into a moral order and Greek rationalism established the relationship between cause and effect. Even though the gods continued to perform prodigious deeds far surpassing the limits of human strength, the Greeks never ascribed these to any mysterious qualities but simply to the inexhaustible will and invincible omnipotence of their gods. Thus, Greek antiquity reduced all things to the scale of human comprehension and laid the foundations of that logical harmony which was always the goal of Greek philosophers.

Dodona, situated in the inhospitable mountains of Epirus, at the foot of Mount Tomarus, seems to this day to bear witness to the omnipresence of the primeval Pelasgian Zeus and the deity of Dione. Dodona is regarded as the cradle of the original Hellenes, whose name is said to be derived from the Sellones, the earliest inhabitants of Dodona. These lived in a harsh country and led a hard life. If Zeus of Olympia represents a highly developed civilization, Zeus of Dodona is a rough, primitive god. The picturesque valley of Olympia in the Peloponnese is called by Pindar 'the mother of the gold-crowned contest'. It lies embedded between the finely proportioned, though not very high, mountain ridges of the Kronos and is watered by the river Cladeus. This is the idyllic landscape in which the Olympic Games were held; according to legend, they were founded by Hercules. They consisted primarily of athletic contests in the arena, but the participants competed not only in physical prowess but also in intellectual and artistic performance. Poets and prose writers would read their works, composers would perform their music. It was at Olympia that Herodotus read from his History, and thus made his famous work public for the first time. The spectators were not Greeks alone—the entire Hellenistic world was assembled there. From the rich settlements on the Mediterranean shores, from the distant regions by the Sea of Azov, from as far as Gibraltar and even from the cold wastes of Scythia, the visitors streamed to Olympia.

While the Hellenized Zeus was venerated at Olympia, Apollo, the god of light and prophecy, was revered at Delphi. This site, the ruins of which contain countless works of art, is in a region of wild grandeur at the foot of Mount Parnassus. According to legend it was at Delphi that Apollo killed the huge dragon Python, symbolizing the victory of light over the powers of darkness and destruction. To house the treasures dedicated to the god, the inhabitants of Athens, of Naxos, of Siphnos, and of other islands erected buildings of great magnificence all round the Temple of Apollo. Like Olympia, Delphi was a magic centre, a place of rapprochement among nations, right down to the days of Theodoric the Great.

Apollo was also the god of the island of Delos. Here Leto had found refuge from Hera, the jealous consort of Zeus, who was hotly pursuing her, and here she gave birth to the twins Apollo and Artemis. Delos, situated not far from Mykonos in the Cyclades, was not only a site dedicated to the cult of the god of light, but also an important centre of ancient shipping and commerce between East and West.

Argos was the site of the famous Temples of Hera. The cult of Hera had spread to the island of Samos and to the city of Perachora on the Isthmus of Corinth in earliest prehistory. In her original Indo-European shape Hera represented the Earth, nourishing its roots, bringing forth plants, and supporting men and beasts. Later she became the goddess of married life and the defender of the matrimonial hearth: she tried to put an end to her faithless husband's escapades by wreaking cruel vengeance upon his paramours—as witnessed by the fate of Semele, Io, and Leto.

Athena, the symbol of wisdom, was venerated at the Acropolis in Athens. It was to her that the Parthenon was dedicated, that most impressive monument of classical antiquity, that magnificent testimony to the Hellenistic splendour of the fifth century B.C. The temple was the work of the famous architects Ictinus and Callicrates and the outstanding sculptor Phidias. Athena's sacred attribute was the owl, that of Zeus the eagle, that of Hera the peacock, and that of Aphrodite the dove. According to Greek legend, Athena sprang fully armed from the head of Zeus, whereas Dionysus, the son of Semele and the god of sacred orgies, sprang from his thigh.

Asclepius, or Aesculapius, the god of medicine, was venerated at several places. The most beautiful of his temples are at Epidaurus in Argolis, at Trikka in Thessaly, and on the island of Cos in the Dodecanese. The sick from all parts of the ancient world made pilgrimages to these temples, to be healed by priests who were the predecessors of our doctors. Treatment was by incantation and invocation of the all-powerful healing god, and also by cures based on practical experience. The snake, associated with knowledge, was one of the symbols of Aesculapius.

Poseidon, the god of the sea, was venerated especially in Morea, in the areas adjacent to the Isthmus of Corinth where the Isthmian Games were held. Other classical games were held at Nemea, where Hercules had killed the legendary lion. The cult of Dionysus goes back to prehistoric times and is thought to have originated in the forests of Thrace; it spread to the whole of Greece and in Attica led to the birth of tragedy. The first manifestation of praise for this god was dithyrambic poetry, a

30 THE GREAT LAVRA   Refectory and well-house

31 MOUNT ATHOS Russian monk and Panteleimon Monastery

33
CHAERONEIA
Memorial
the battle fought
in 338 B.C.

34   MARATHON   The battlefield of 490 B.C.

35 HYDRA Between the Saronian Sea and the Gulf of Argolis

sacred hymn to Bacchus, the god of grapes and wine. From this early form developed the tragedy, that most perfect literary genre of classical antiquity.

Demeter, the personification of earth, and her daughter Persephone, as the queen of the underworld, represented the deities of Eleusis. The deepest meaning of the Eleusinian Mysteries remains largely unsolved, as does that of the mysteries of the Karabeiri in Samothrace. Arcadia, the realm of Pan, the god of woods and shepherds, was also the region where Artemis, the virgin goddess of the hunt, roamed over hill and dale. Artemis was venerated also at Ephesus, where her temple was one of the Seven Wonders of the World before Herostratus set fire to it. Artemis was originally represented by moonlight, and later became identified with the moon just as her brother Apollo became identified with the sun.

Hestia was the patron goddess of domestic bliss; Ares was the god of war. Aphrodite, the goddess of love and eternal youth, was venerated particularly in the southeastern part of the Mediterranean region, in the islands off the Asia Minor coast and in Cyprus, where, as Anadyomene, she had emerged from the sea near Paphos. Hermes, the messenger of the gods, was the patron of commerce and the god of oratory; he also conducted the souls of the dead into Hades, the realm ruled over by Pluto.

The Hellenistic Pantheon was the seat of numerous gods, demons, and spirits around which an elaborate tissue of legends was spun. Yet these legends can be seen to contain many eternal truths and to reflect, often very subtly, the experiences of human life. The people to whom they are ascribed were clearly intent on perpetuating that which they saw as the enduring substance of human existence. The basic subject matter might have remained of purely folklore interest; its artistic transformation, however, reflects a tremendous wealth of ideas and great profundity of thought. Thus the legend of Prometheus, 'the first political prisoner in history', did not gain its full moral significance until the all-embracing mind of Aeschylus invested the parable with universal significance.

Historical Destiny

Greek history owes the fact that it is richer than that of most nations principally to
the resilience of the Hellenes. Unlike Accadians, Elamites, Hittites and Avars, they
did not allow their cultural heritage and national consciousness to be destroyed by
their countless invaders, but invariably remembered their origins and preserved their
national awareness, regardless of the ordeals which beset them. Certainly their way of
thinking has changed over the centuries and is different today from that of their ancestors. Even so, common characteristics can be seen in many fields, testifying to the
continuity which links the present day with classical antiquity.

An important part in Greek history was played by geographical position. The
numerous island groups, representing the major part of the national territory, have
always been of outstanding importance as centres of maritime communications and
as a constant bridge between the three continents of the ancient and medieval world.
The original inhabitants of Crete, and after them the Greeks, were the unchallenged
rulers of the seas. They extended the boundaries of their empire and consolidated
it. While the Phoenicians confined themselves to setting up trade ports and shipping centres, the Greeks established powerful institutions of great durability. Towards the end of the second and at the beginning of the first pre-Christian millennium they established vigorous colonies along most of the Mediterranean shores—on
the Black Sea, on the coasts of Asia Minor, in the lands of southern Italy and in
Sicily.

No definite evidence is available about the movements of Hellenic tribes into the
areas in which they became permanently settled. What is certain is that, in the course
of the second millennium B.C., Indo-Europeans invaded the south-eastern Mediterranean region, occupied it, and settled in the places in which they were subsequently to
develop their civilizing activity—first the Achaeans, followed by Ionians, Aeolians
and Dorians. These people soon displayed distinctive characteristics and abilities,

even though they belonged to the same race. By the end of the twelfth pre-Christian century these population movements were virtually completed.

The fusion of the Achaeans with the original population of Greece gave rise to the first Mycenaean civilization from 1700 B.C. to 1400 B.C. In that phase the influence of the Cretans on all aspects of the life of the mainland populations was considerable. In the late Mycenaean period, 1400–1200 B.C., that influence diminished, while at the same time the power of the Achaeans was consolidated. Important relics of the power of the second Mycenaean period are being found today at Mycenae and at Tiryns in the Peloponnese. Until late in the nineteenth century the so-called Mycenaean civilization was thought to have existed only in Homer's imagination. But in 1868 the existence of the historical city of Troy was proved, and excavations in Mycenae, Tiryns and Orchomenos have since irrefutably proved the historical existence of the Homeric world.

After the fall of Mycenae, Argos became the leading city-state, and during the first half of the seventh century B.C. guided the destinies of the Greeks under the rule of the powerful King Pheidon, who invented the scales and introduced a unified system of weights and measures. After his death Argos fell apart; it was the turn of Sparta to seize power in the Peloponnese and gradually to assume the dominant position throughout Greece. The Spartan way of life was based on frugality, militarism, extreme patriotism and contempt of death; Spartans also rejected anything which might impede their rigorous rationalism.

While Sparta reflected Doric traits, Athens, developing at the same time, owed its flourishing artistic and intellectual life to the Ionian spirit. Since Homer was regarded as a citizen of Smyrna, the creation of the epic, of philosophy and of historiography can in fact be attributed to the Ionians of Asia Minor. Asia Minor also produced Thales, Anaxagoras, Heraclitus, Anaximander and Anaximenes, as well as Hecataeus, the precursor of the Dorian Herodotus. In Attica the Ionians practised the drama: Thespis, Aeschylus, Sophocles, and Euripides wrote their classical tragedies, and Aristophanes was the most celebrated writer of comedies in Athens.

The power of Athens rested upon her domination of the seas. The civilization of ancient Greece, the foundations of modern humanism, are predominantly of Ionian—*i.e.*, Athenian—origin. In the fifth and fourth centuries B.C. Athens was the heart of the civilized world and practised an almost magical influence upon all intellectual endeavour. This 'Hellenistic miracle' flourished for several decades, from about 490 to 400 B.C. It is above all to Pericles, the outstanding statesman, that the Grecian world owes that decisive official support for the arts, literature, and architecture (witness the building of the Acropolis) and the rise of Athens to world fame.

The envy of Sparta and its imprudent policies eventually led to the Peloponnesian War which continued for twenty-seven years and ended with Athens' defeat at the hands of Sparta. This contest brought great losses to the Greek population, devastated their country and reduced Athens to the position of a second-rate power. It emerged so weakened from this fratricidal struggle that it could not even think of regaining its former position by its own strength. This situation was not altered even by the short-lived hegemony of the Thebans. Profiting from the changing political groupings and balances between the Greek city states, Macedonia, to the north of Greece, succeeded in assuming the leadership of the Hellenistic world. That country had been reorganized by King Philip II. His son Alexander set about realizing his father's bold plan: he launched his gigantic campaign which aimed at no less than the annihilation of the Persian kings. This elimination of the constant danger from the Medes was, in a sense, Europe's counter-blow at Asia. Alexander led his armies to the coast of the Troad, fought a battle on the river Granicus, crossed Phrygia, subjected Asia Minor, conquered Egypt, Syria and Babylon, and reached the Persian Gulf. Shortly afterwards he began his great drive into faraway India, using for this campaign the armies which he raised in the countries conquered by him.

48

When Alexander died in Babylon in 323 B.C., at the age of thirty-three, his empire broke up, and the separate fragments became new Greek states. The dynasty of the Ptolemies seized Egypt, that of the Seleucids seized Syria, the Attalids established their rule over Pergamum, while Antipater and his descendants continued to rule over Macedonia and the Greek mainland. Thus began the new, so-called Hellenistic, epoch. Greek became the common language of the Mediterranean region. Many nations adopted Greek culture and this, in consequence, spread as far as Afghanistan, Baluchistan, and Hindustan. It was this largely unified culture that was so important in preparing the way for the Roman Empire which was to embrace so many regions a few centuries later.

In Latium there arose a military power comparable to Sparta, which by force of arms spread over the Italian peninsula and thrust outwards in all directions of the ancient world. Crushing all resistance in her neighbouring territories, Rome toppled the small Grecian principalities in southern Italy and Sicily, and destroyed Carthage—though not without having suffered many painful wounds in the course of Hannibal's campaigns.

The rise of the peoples of Epirus under King Pyrrhus was only short-lived. Rome subjected Epirus, Macedonia and Thrace, and eventually advanced into the Greek heartland. The destruction of Corinth by Lucius Mummius in 146 B.C. meant the end of Greece's rôle in history; the country was placed under Roman rule as a province under the name of Achaia. Greek moral and intellectual influence, however, continued to gain in importance and led to the development of a Greco-Roman civilization which lasted into the Byzantine age.

The beginnings of Christianity meant a turning-point in the destiny of Greece. The new religion, sprung up and grown strong in a Hellenized world, was radiating outwards by means of the Greek language. The great upheavals of the age of the Roman emperors, which led to the fall of the Western Roman Empire in A.D. 476, paved the way for a revival of Hellenism.

Constantine the Great, in deciding to set up a new Rome on the boundary of Asia and Europe, was clearly motivated by military considerations since the Roman possessions in Asia and Africa were enormous. What the Emperor could not know was that the foundation of his city, later to be known as Constantinople, also ushered in a new period of history.

After the fall of the Western Roman Empire it was Eastern Rome—*i.e.*, Byzantium—that took over the government and defence of the western provinces. Although Hellenism was fairly well developed in the Eastern-Roman Empire of Justinian in the sixth century, it became all-pervasive a hundred years later. Asia Minor, moreover, proved an inexhaustible source for reinforcing the Greco-Christian character of the Empire. It was just about then that Islam first attempted to conquer these regions, and the repulse of these attacks was now the responsibility of the Christianized Greeks. Under the leadership of the Isaurians, a dynasty from Asia Minor, they succeeded in averting the Islamic threat in the eighth century.

The Byzantine Empire came into being in A.D. 330, under Constantine I, and ended in 1453 with the conquest of Constantinople by the Turks. During this turbulent and often savage period there was no lack of usurpers to the throne or of hostile incursions. Equally numerous, however, were the instances of heroism and chivalry, in spite of the unceasing struggle in which the people were engaged. The Byzantine Empire knew only too well that it was envied and beset by enemies, but it was always aware of its dual mission—to preserve the classical civilization inherited from Greece and to be a beacon radiating the spirit of Christianity. Throughout eleven centuries the Byzantine Empire had been the great guiding star of the nations. In the end, its fall was brought about by the Crusaders, in particular by the Fourth Crusade which was called off in front of the walls of Constantinople, its religious aims unfulfilled. The Crusaders gave up all ideas of penetrating farther into Asia where their predecessors had suffered such heavy losses. Instead, in 1204, they decided to capture Constantinople. Having captured and sacked it, they founded the Latin Empire of the

50

Baldwins. This Frankish occupation was soon extended over the whole of Greece. A few states attempted to resist the attack—as, for instance, the empire of Nicaea, which for a while even succeeded in reconquering Constantinople. Others, however, like the despotism of Epirus, the empire of Trebizond, and the principality of Morea, were unable to escape military and political collapse. The Venetians had secured their positions on the Greek coasts and islands, and so skilfully extended their power that the Turks had to wage protracted wars against them before forcing them to yield some of their conquests. On the Ionian islands Venice maintained its rule until they were occupied by the British, after the fall of Napoleon Bonaparte.

The eighteenth century was a period of enlightenment for Greece. The great educators awakened among their people memories of the civilization of their ancestors; they prepared the Greeks for their rising, which broke out in 1821 and aimed at national independence. The heroic deeds performed by the Greek people in this conflict can bear comparison with the heroism of their ancestors in antiquity and in the Middle Ages. The war ended in 1829 with the liberation of a small part of the Hellenistic territory; this part achieved recognition as an autonomous state by Russia, Britain, and France.

This liberated Greek nation rallied, consolidated its existence as a social and national nucleus, and endeavoured to liberate the remaining Hellenistic territories from Osman rule. After an inevitable string of successes and reverses, this modern Greek nation grew from a population of 800,000 in 1831 to the present-day state with a population of over eight million.

The milestones in modern Greek history which deserve mention are the incorporation in Greece of the seven Ionian islands, achieved in agreement with Queen Victoria; the liberation of Epirus, Macedonia, Thrace, Crete, and the Aegean Islands, as a result of the Balkan wars; the cession to Greece of Thessaly and the Epirot territories around the town of Arta; and Greece's leap into Asia Minor, on the basis of the Treaty of Sèvres, which granted her Smyrna and some of its hinterland.

Greece and the Sea

Greece belongs to the mainland of the Balkan peninsula and, at the same time, is a collection of islands in the south-eastern Mediterranean. Throughout history Greece shared the destinies of the Balkan countries, of Western Europe, and of the people who had settled on her coasts, along her extensive sea routes, and on her islands. The Greek race's love of the sea has remained unchanged through the ages, and the country's economy has always been inseparably bound up with it.

In earliest antiquity the Cretans challenged the Phoenicians' commercial hegemony of the sea. The Mycenaeans, at a later date, set out from the Gulf of Argolis, crossed the Aegean Sea in all directions, and established regular trade relations with the Cretans. In the classical age the Athenian democracy was a powerful island state. The 'wooden walls' which the ambiguous oracle of Delphi had advised the Athenians to rely on for their safety, and which Themistocles had correctly interpreted to mean ships, saved Athens from the Persian threat in the naval battle of Salamis.

Nearchus, the admiral of Alexander the Great, led the Greek fleet as far afield as the Persian Gulf. The Byzantines invented 'Greek fire', which they hurled at enemy ships by means of catapults. In more modern days, when pirates were terrorizing the Mediterranean with their pillaging raids, armed Greek ships went out to engage them and re-established law and order.

Both under Turkish rule and after the achievement of political independence, shipping was an important source of revenue for the Greeks. The principal bases of their merchant fleet then were the harbour of Galaxidion in the Gulf of Corinth, the islands of Syra in the Cyclades and Leucas in the Ionian Sea, the city of Aetolikon on the Mesolongion promontory, the island of Chios off the Asia Minor coast, Cos in the Dodecanese, and Sciathus in the northern Sporades. A very large number of sailing ships of all kinds, manned by bold seafarers, ventured as far as the Black Sea ports, the Middle East, the coast of North Africa, and the Adriatic.

39
EASTERN
CRETE
Peasant
woman
threshing
grain

40
CHIOS
After
church

44 PAROS Ancient columnar drums used in medieval
fortress walls

45 NAXOS Rough-hewn statue

46 PAROS
Bells among the branches
of a tree

47 PAROS
Fishing port of Naussa

The ancient centres of Greek shipping are now forgotten. But dim memories of former glory survive among the people, and a small maritime museum at Galaxidion houses a great many interesting relics from an age which will never return.

The inhabitants of the island of Calymnos in the Dodecanese engage in sponge-fishing to this day and derive a reasonable livelihood from it. During the first days of spring they hold their traditional religious festivities; then the fishermen sail their barges out of port and set course for the north coasts of Africa, off Sfax and Benghazi. From this voyage they do not return until several months later, but then their boats are heavily laden with precious sponges. These are processed on Calymnos and then exported to the Greek mainland and to many foreign countries. Unfortunately, several fishermen lose their lives every year while engaged in this dangerous work, usually as a result of being overcome by diver's sickness and drowning.

In every country engaging in marine shipping the transition from sail to steam meant an economic and social revolution on a considerable scale; this was true also of Greece. This irresistible development, with which the Greek shipowners managed to keep pace, resulted, among other things, in the emergence of the Piraeus as the major port of the country and as one of the principal commercial centres of the Mediterranean. In the league table of the world's merchant navies Greece holds sixth place, after Japan. If we disregard Liberia, whose flag is principally used by ships belonging to other countries, Greece is seen holding fifth place and to be developing still in all aspects of modern high-sea shipping. From the Far East to northern Scandinavia, Greek ships sail all the world's seas and oceans. The names of several Greek shipowning families have become household words. They represent veritable shippers' dynasties and have interests in all key centres of world trade—in London, New York, Halifax, Sydney, Hamburg, and in the Piraeus.

The number of Greek merchant ships in 1964 was 1412 with a total tonnage of 7,155,270. Moreover, a large number of Greek-owned ships sail under so-called flags of convenience—because of considerable tax advantages—especially under the flags of Panama, Liberia, and Honduras. If we include these units, the total number increases to roughly 2400 with a cargo capacity of approximately 20,000,000 tons. These figures illustrate the exceptional importance which merchant shipping holds for the Greek economy.

On the eve of the Second World War the Greek merchant navy consisted of 577 units; in 1945 the figure was down to 140. One of Greece's greatest achievements in the field of merchant shipping since the end of the war was the creation of a huge fleet of giant tankers. At the end of 1964 this fleet comprised 36 ships of 30,000 G. R. T., 32 of 22,000 G. R. T., and 526 ranging from 9000 to 22,500 G. R. T. At the same time, passenger liners were built on a growing scale for domestic services, as well as larger vessels for the transatlantic routes on which Greece had achieved world fame. With some 54,000 crew members on Greek ships and some 26,000 on foreign vessels, Greece today continues her glorious naval tradition. This is not only a source of national pride but also one of increasing revenue.

Another important factor in the Greek economy is fishing. Although the fishermen have at their disposal the most up-to-date equipment, they continue, somewhat surprisingly, to cling to often very primitive tackle which, even at best, can ensure only moderate catches. Fishing, in consequence, is by no means as profitable as might be expected or as it should be considering the length of the country's coastline. Paradoxically as it may seem, Greece frequently suffers from a shortage of fish even though the fishing grounds in Greek waters are plentiful.

The inadequacy of the fishing industry is due, to some extent at least, to the irregular configuration of the sea floor near the coasts. The frequent and sudden breaks in the weather also represent an obstacle to efficiency. Nevertheless, the majority of fishing-boats are employed in coastal fishing; these are so simple that their operation represents no problem. More than 6000 fishing-boats supply fish to some 40,000 people for whom this is their main diet; even so this yield represents barely 10 per cent of the annual national production. Far greater efficiency is achieved by mechanical fishing which, with a total of over 100,000 tons, accounts for roughly 60 per cent of the annual Greek catch.

For the past twenty years Greece has tried to offset the inadequate yield of its inshore fishing industry by developing long-distance fishing. Fishing in overseas waters, moreover, was expected to result in lower prices. A fleet of twenty-three big fishing-trawlers with refrigeration equipment is nowadays engaged in large-scale fishing off the African Rio de Oro coast as far afield as Dakar. From there the fish is supplied to the world markets in vast quantities.

Aegean Asia Minor

The Hellespont

The broad peninsula of Asia Minor extends roughly in the shape of a rectangle in an east-westerly direction. In the north it is bounded by the Black Sea and the Sea of Marmara. Towards the western end of the Sea of Marmara its northern and southern coastlines approach each other more and more closely until, at the north-western point of Asia Minor, they form the straits of the Hellespont, more commonly known nowadays as the Dardanelles.

The name Hellespont goes back to ancient mythology: it refers to the deep lake of Helle, the beautiful daughter of King Athamas of Thessaly. Riding on the winged ram with the golden fleece, Helle lost her balance and plunged into the sapphire-blue, foaming waters of the strait and was drowned. It was through this very Hellespont that Jason sailed his fast ship, the Argo, in search of just that golden fleece. In earliest antiquity the story was already being told of how Hero of Sestos, the charming young priestess of Aphrodite, the goddess of love, had followed her drowned lover, Leander of Abydos, into the deadly sea. Xerxes, the powerful King of the Persians, here scourged the waves after his fleet, all lined up for the conquest of Greece, had suffered shipwreck in the treacherous currents. Many a time the destinies of mankind were decided at the Hellespont.

The importance of this legendary spot of Asia Minor probably dates back to the story of Troy and the *Iliad*. The characters of the Trojan war and their feats have remained part of our cultural heritage to this day, even though they have faded a little over the centuries. Yet is there a more moving scene anywhere than Hector's parting from Andromache?

To the west of the Hellespont glistened and gleamed the boundless sea which was everything to the Mediterranean world—the 'wine-dark sea' which linked ancient Crete with Troy, and Troy with the whole world. The Mediterranean was the delight of the antique world. It was present symbolically in Homer's blue chalice, in the blue sails of the triremes, and in the diaphanous gorgeous blue robes of Aphrodite. To this day the Mediterranean, together with the famous historic sites along its endless coasts, remains an inexhaustible source of pleasure.

From an ethnological point of view the Mediterranean represents the sixth continent. The conventional geographical division of the earth's land masses into five continents is entirely arbitrary. Can one really maintain that the Mediterranean is surrounded by three different continents? Surely not: basically they are all Mediterranean countries. Asia does not start until we reach the Iranian plateau. Egypt and Algeria are not Africa—the black continent begins only with the Sahara. Moreover, Greece, Italy, Spain or Marseilles belong far less to the rest of Europe than they do to the Mediterranean. The moment people settle on the coasts of this sea they fall victim to the indefinable magic of this particular part of the world: they become Mediterranean. The Mare Nostrum of the chauvinistic Romans was, in fact, a sea at the hub of civilization. Many of all the most valuable things that have been written or created, and which have survived to our day, originated on its historic coasts.

The eastern coasts of the Mediterranean, in particular, represent a single integral cultural region. Whereas other parts of the world can boast, at best, of a few separate civilizations, the eastern Mediterranean countries assimilated in turn those of the Sumerians, Babylonians, Assyrians, Egyptians, Hittites, Minoans, Persians, and Greeks.

The cradle of mankind may perhaps have stood in central Asia. From there, the early tribes were compelled to emigrate when, after the Ice Age, the earth's surface began to dry up. Other reasons for this explosive spread of populations were no doubt an increasing population density and a lust for booty. Neighbours in more fertile countries were attacked and expropriated. In this way numerous population movements of the earliest periods developed into campaigns of conquest.

One of the earliest trouble-makers was Turkestan. The peoples of the Urals and the Altay mountains drove their neighbouring tribes in front of them, as they had been accustomed to do with their herds since time immemorial. They intermixed with all people who came under their rule and thus became the founders of the Sumerian civilization, a blend of the most diverse races. True human culture was never the monopoly of a single race.

Since earliest prehistoric times Asia Minor, and later Syria and Palestine, were repeatedly invaded by waves of people coming from the north, the north-east, and the east. A few ethnic waves swept from Turkestan southward through Transcaucasia, Armenia, Asia Minor, and Syria as far as Arabia; some of them even crossed the isthmus of Suez and reached Africa. Another of these periodic migrations aimed westward and brought the Mesopotamian civilization to the Aegean shores of Asia Minor.

Owing to its geographical situation Asia Minor thus became an exceedingly important transit route for early population movements. The other peninsulas of the Mediterranean—Italy, Greece, and Spain—all run from north to south. But Asia Minor extends from east to west. Because of its situation at the intersection of Europe, Asia and Africa it became a bridge between these three continents and the main highway for migrating tribes or campaigns of conquest—most of them moving in a westerly direction and getting as far as the Aegean coast.

From the Hellespont this coast turns southward, forming a number of major or lesser bays, divided by mountainous promontories, spits of land, and capes. The spurs of one of these submerged promontories formed a group of islands, the Sporades or Cyclades, sometimes called the Archipelago for short. The last term is quite justified: archipelago means 'ancient sea' and even the early Egyptians had described them as 'the islands at the heart of the sea'. Where else was the heart of the sea to be found? This is the genuine world of Homer, who was very probably born either at Colophon, on Chios, or in Izmir (Smyrna).

The most southerly spur of Asia Minor, which alternately rises from the sea and dips back into it, consists of a string of islands—Rhodes, Cos, and Carpathus. The nations which, coming from the east, had moved across Asia Minor then used these islands as springboards for Crete. There, in Crete, they produced the Minoan and Aegean civilizations which were soon to spread throughout the Mediterranean region. Thus we find the two-headed Anatolian axe, the *labrys,* not only in Crete, but also in Babylon and in Syria.

Anatolia

Asia Minor must have been the scene of hectic human activity even in prehistoric times. With a coast of some 2000 miles facing a warm, navigable sea, the country had become a shipping centre for considerable parts of the ancient world at a very early date. Excavations in central Anatolia have revealed archives of Sumero-Accadian trading colonies founded at Kadesh near Caesarea in the latter half of the third pre-Christian millennium. The tablets show that an invasion of Babylon was essential at one stage to defend the rights of these colonies.

At the beginning of the second pre-Christian millennium the war chariots of the Hittites swept into Asia Minor which was then a world of many languages and of a high level of civilization. The Hittites conquered the Kingdom of Hatti and settled on the river Halys in the land of the Amazons. The Hittite tribes spoke six languages—due to their intermingling with the earlier inhabitants. This fact proves that Asia Minor had been inhabited by heterogeneous elements even before the Hittites—the Mitanni, the Harreri, the Kassites, the wild Kaski of Lesser Armenia, the Artava, and the Levites. Records of the early Egyptian kings Thutmose III and Amenhotep II mention the Keftiu—that is the Minoan Cretans who were in full possession of the Aegean civilization in the third pre-Christian millennium. Having originally emigrated to Crete from Asia Minor, they had settlements on both sides of the Aegean Sea. Egypt maintained friendly relations with the Minoans, the 'island people'. About 1400 B. C. their name suddenly disappears from Egyptian literature and another nation is mentioned, 'the sea people', especially the Shirdanu.

50 IOS Upper town

51 IOS Chapels and terraced vineyards

52
IOS
Street with
passageway

53
PATMOS
Byzantine chapel

54
PATMOS
Harbour of
Scala,
seen from
the monastery

55
PATMOS
Cave of
St. John the
Divine

Led by their emperor Mutallis, the Hittites fought a battle against the Pharaoh Rameses II near Kadesh in Palestine in the year 1296 B.C. Among the Hittites' Anatolian allies the Shirdanu, the Danuna, the Lukki, the Mysians, the Dardanoi, and the Cilicians are listed. The Shirdanu or Sardani emigrated to Sardinia and gave that island its present name. The Danuna are identical with Homer's Danaoi. They came originally from the area of Adana, as has been proved by excavations there. The Lukki are the Lycians, from the birthplace of Apollo. The Dardanoi inhabited the region of the Dardanelles, and the Mysians were the people on the shore of the Sea of Marmara. Later a coalition was formed between Lycians, Shirdanu, Shakalash, Achaivasha, and Tursha, which in turn formed an alliance with the Libyans of North Africa with a view to mounting pillaging campaigns into Egypt.

These were still relatively calm days for Asia Minor, compared with the turbulent population movements which were soon to sweep over the peninsula. The inscriptions of Medinet Habu give us an idea of the chaos which reigned here at the beginning of the first millennium B.C. Throughout the peninsula empires collapsed like packs of cards. One people after another emigrated to escape the famine and the wars of the peninsula. The events of that period, however, are still veiled in impenetrable darkness, and historians are reduced to speculation and hypotheses. New tribes are mentioned in the reports of the battle of Kadesh. Fighting alongside the Anatolian auxiliaries were the Pulesati, the Shakalash, and the Zakala. They were defeated by Rameses III both on land and on the sea. These Pulesati are the Philistines of Hebrew history, who were settled principally in Philistia and gave their name to Palestine. The Zakala and the Pulesati are both of Creto-Carian origin.

During the reign of the great Pharaoh Akhenaton certain Aramaic tribes from Tell el-Amarna, who called themselves Kabiru, invaded Palestine. As they were of Semitic origin and their language was closely related to that of the Hebrews, it is assumed that they were the predecessors of the later Hebrews who settled in Palestine and became the unwelcome neighbours of the Canaanites. But Asia Minor was not simply a transit route for all these people. Many of them settled and merged with the indigenous inhabitants.

In the earliest prehistoric sources dating back to the mythological age the original inhabitants of Asia Minor, the Aegean islands and the eastern part of Greece are referred to as Pelasgians, the 'sea people'. They belonged to the Mediterranean race and must have sprung from a mixture of all the peoples mentioned above. They spoke their own non-Greek language. Herodotus describes the Spartans of Greece as Hellenes, but the Athenians as Pelasgians.

The earliest history of Greece is, of course, pure mytho-theology. Nevertheless, some of the myths—as, for instance, that of Deucalion, the common ancestor of the Greeks —contain a nucleus of historical truth. Wrathful Zeus decides to send a flood upon the earth. Deucalion, forewarned by his father Prometheus, builds an ark. As the waters recede the ark makes its landfall on Mount Parnassus. This myth has the same origin as the Biblical one of Noah and his ark. Both are probably rooted in a memory of the great Mesopotamian flood of the third millennium B.C. Settlers must have reached Greece from Mesopotamia, via Asia Minor and the Aegean islands or down the Balkan Peninsula. All Pelasgian, Achaean, Mycenaean, and Dorian incursions and immigrations into Greece were waves of westerly population movements lasting several centuries. Archaeological research has shown that Homer's Danaoi, presumably the ancient Achaeans, were of Anatolian origin.

The Ionians, on the other hand, are mentioned in the Pentateuch as Javanians, descended from Javan, the son of Japheth. About the fifteenth or sixteenth century B.C. the Persians called them the Iauna. The word Iavanes or Iavones later became Iones. As the sons of Apollo, the Ionians laid claim to divine descent. But the god Apollo originally belonged to a very ancient matriarchal civilization of Asia Minor. In the *Iliad* he is still an enemy of the Achaians and eventually kills Achilles. Homer calls Apollo Lykegenes—*i.e.*, the one born in Lycia. His earliest four sanctuaries, all of them much older than Delphi, are on the Aegean coast of Anatolia—the sacred sites

62

of Gryneium, Clarus, Didyma, and Patara. The spread of the Apollo mythology therefore traces the path followed by the Ionians in their westward migrations.

The Trojan war took place from about 1200 to 1180 B.C. It marks a turning-point in the history of mankind. About a century later entire hordes of Phrygians poured from the Balkan countries across to Asia Minor and settled in the north-western part of the peninsula where they took over the heritage of the Hittites. After a further century these Phrygians were themselves flooded by an assault of the savage Cimmerii and almost completely wiped out. A few decades later the Lydians, a people of very high civilization with their capital at Sardes, defeated the Cimmerii. Then followed a relatively calm period, broken only by lesser incursions of Scythians and other tribes along the Aegean coast. After that began the earliest period of classical antiquity. It is to this dawn of history that we must look for the beginnings of human civilization in the modern meaning of the word.

Each time a tribe swept through Asia Minor in an east-westerly direction some splinter group would be caught up along the Aegean coastal hem of Anatolia and would there merge with the local inhabitants. In addition, population movements across the Aegean Sea cannot be excluded either. These Aegeo-Anatolians were called Aeolians, Ionians, and Carians, but these names have little more than geographical meaning. Each language had its own viability and power of expansion, often independently of the political or military power of its speakers. Greek, as a more highly developed language, soon predominated in the coastal areas of Asia Minor. The successful amalgamation of peoples of different origin also mitigated the harshness of conflicting philosophies, religions and traditions, and eventually ironed them out completely.

Hittites, Phrygians, Lydians, Carians, and Lycians transmitted to the Aegeo-Anatolians the culture which they themselves had received from the east. These Anatolians had no gods which could have imposed upon them sacred and unassailable moral laws. Thus, for the first time in human history, the intellect was set free to interpret the universe, untrammelled by priestly or kingly interests. Thales of Miletus, living in the seventh century B.C., accurately calculated and predicted the solar eclipse of 28th May 585 B.C. Such an outstanding achievement could only have been the product of knowledge accumulated over the centuries. Thus Europe owes its science, its literature freed from hieratic traditions, and its laws framed with a view to the common interest, essentially to western Asia Minor.

Assos

From Troy a road winds southwards through the valley of the Scamander, the river mentioned by Homer, and passes through the village of Ayvacik. In the Bay of Adramyttia, about twelve miles from the beautiful Cape Lefkon, it reaches the ruins of ancient Assos. All that is left of this ancient city is crowded together high up along the edges of a few steep scarps rising from the coast like a gigantic stairway. From the heights of the city one's gaze sweeps over the sea to the island of Mytilene, the birthplace of Sappho of Lesbos. Assos covers an area of one square mile and its walls in places rise to a height of sixty-two feet. On the acropolis, the 'high city', the ruins of a temple which was presumably sacred to Athena lie scattered about the ground. The colonnades of the *agora* and a theatre, on the other hand, are well preserved.

Tulhalias IV, King of the Hittites, came to Assos to suppress a rebellion by a few Aegean cities in a region referred to as Assuva. Assuva was the original name of Ephesus; the Egyptians called the city Iasia, which presumably was also the name of the goddess Artemis of Ephesus. This name was taken over by the Lydians, and in the form 'Asia' came to be applied to the western part of Anatolia. In Roman days the entire Anatolian peninsula was called the Province of Asia. Not till the fifth century A.D., when the term Asia came to be applied to the continent as a whole, did the Byzantines add the adjective minor to distinguish Anatolia, now Asia Minor,

64

from the remainder of the continent. Anatolia means 'the land of the rising sun'. An earlier name of Assos was Pedassos. Topographical names ending in '-ssos', such as Parnassos and Halikarnassos (Parnassus and Halicarnassus), belong to a very ancient Anatolian language. This suggests that a city must have stood at this spot not later than towards the end of the second pre-Christian millennium.

It is assumed that a group of Aeolian expatriates, fleeing from Greece after the Doric invasion, settled here at the end of the second pre-Christian millennium. The name is attested as that of an Ionian settlement in Anatolia. But there is no historical evidence whatever that it was a Doric invasion that destroyed the Mycenaean civilization. The rapid collapse of the Mycenaean empire is just as inexplicable as the sudden disappearance of the Hittites in Asia Minor or of the Minoans in Crete. Greece, Asia Minor, and Italy are volcanic countries with periodic earthquakes. Even in historic times entire towns have been wiped out and levelled to the ground by such natural disasters. What has sometimes been described as a Doric invasion, therefore, may equally well have been an emigration movement or a gradual drift of Dorians into a new uninhabited region.

All reports about the Doric invasion and a subsequent forced settlement of Ionians and Aeolians in the midst of Carian and Lelegian tribes on the Anatolian coast go back to ancient authors and are largely founded on myths. In the second half of the last century, however, these accounts were regarded as authentic and incorporated in the accepted teaching of ancient history. However, Achaeans had been founding colonies on the Anatolian coast of the Aegean Sea long before those controversial Doric raids and had become intermingled with the local inhabitants. They were a great sea-faring nation, with the result that the Aegean civilization became the first truly maritime civilization of the ancient world.

The Temple of Assos, seen as a place where pagan gods had been worshipped, was totally destroyed in the Byzantine period. The shattered columns cluttering the site are a symbol of the transience of all human civilizations. But beyond Assos gleams the ancient, the eternal Mediterranean, witness to so many empires and civilizations. Cleanthes, Zeno's successor as the head of the Stoics, was a native of this city. There exists a fine pantheistic hymn to Zeus, which praises him no longer as a god in the mythological sense but as a spiritual being pervading and governing the entire universe.

Isolated olive trees are found almost everywhere in Anatolia—but here at Assos they occur as a dense forest across which the Aegean winds blow, producing one silver ripple after another. In antiquity a road led westwards from the Hellespont, across the plain of Antandrus and Adramittium, over to Pergamum and then along the Aeolian coast as far as Gryneium, Myrina, Kyme, Larissa, and Smyrna to the Ionian city of Ephesus, past many ancient cities whose names to this day are full of magic.

Pergamum

In the midst of this region, surrounded by olive groves, rises the impressive acropolis of Pergamum. The name—Pergamon in its Greek form—comes from a forgotten language of Asia Minor and means fortress or castle. The Greeks took over the term, and Homer refers to the Pergamum of Troy in southern Asia Minor. The site of Pergamum was already settled in the later Stone Age, as witnessed by finds of neolithic battle-axes. In ancient mythology it is a famous town under the name of Teuthrania. Xenophon describes it as impregnable. We know for certain that it struck its own coins as early as 420 B.C.

In this fortress city Lysimachus, a general of Alexander the Great, stored up all the treasures he had collected, as the spoils of war, in the course of his royal master's campaigns against the Persians, and entrusted them to the care of Phileterius, one of his officers. Lysimachus was later defeated in battle by Seleucus and killed at Magnesia. Phileterius seized the gold and proclaimed himself an independent ruler. Thus he

66

founded the dynasty of the Kings of Pergamum in the third century B.C. He was succeeded by two rulers by the name of Eumenes and three by the name of Attalus. Eumenes I won a brilliant victory over Antiochus II at Sardis; Attalus I defeated the Galatians, and Pergamum became an ally of Rome. Under the reign of Attalus II it was the cultural capital of an extensive territory, as the frontiers of his kingdom, though founded in western Asia Minor, had been pushed forward then as far as the Taurus mountains. The last King of Pergamum, Attalus III, so loved his wife that on her death, in a fit of despair, he gave his empire away to Rome. Rome, needless to say, was not slow to accept the gift with due gratitude.

For two centuries Pergamum, along with Ephesus and Smyrna, was one of the three great cities of western Anatolia. It became the favourite winter residence of the Roman emperors and thus a centre of emperor worship. Later, it was at Pergamum that one of the first seven Christian churches in Asia Minor was founded. The acropolis was converted into a fortress by the Byzantines, who regarded all monuments of the antique city as blasphemous pagan structures. The classical age was definitely over; Pergamum lost its importance under Byzantine rule. During their advance to Constantinople the Arabs conquered the city and throughout the twelfth century it was part of the Seljuk empire of Konia. By building mosques and caravanserais the Seljuk rulers tried to recapture Pergamum's former prosperity, but the city's glorious days were too clearly linked with the classical age.

At Priene, in the valley of the Maeander, we can see the first instance of an ancient city laid out in accordance with modern principles of town planning. It was designed by the famous architect Hippodamus of Miletus as a grid of roads intersecting at right angles, with regular rectangular blocks of buildings between the intersections. The public buildings, too, were arranged in a row alongside each other. This then was already a functionally planned city. But Pergamum regarded this chequer-board plan as rather monotonous and opposed to it its own so-called royal or ornamental style which visualizes the whole city as a single magnificent monument. These two principles, already found in ancient Anatolian town planning, are still the subject of controversy among town planners today.

The upper city of Pergamum, the acropolis, had four principal and several lesser terraces which imparted to the city the impressive appearance of a Babylonian tower. In the north the city was framed by the well-watered Ida range, where the Olympian gods resided and gazed down, on the far side, upon ancient Troy. In the second century B.C. this acropolis far surpassed that of Athens. (Pergamum even exported its artists to Athens.) The topmost terrace was adorned with palaces, temples, an extensive library, and a theatre. Today one enters the theatre through the ruins of the Temple of Athena and is overwhelmed by the magnificent view, the harmony of the buildings and the glorious scenic backdrop behind. Here, in this theatre of Pergamum, movable stage sets were first used. On the lower terraces were two agoras, an altar dedicated to Zeus in commemoration of the victory over the Galatians, a Temple of Demeter—a veritable architectural gem in the Aeolian style—public baths, three magnificent gymnasia, and other public buildings, which made Pergamum the cradle of Hellenistic art. The city was not just the capital of a country but the centre of an entire civilization, in the same way that Miletus, Ephesus, and Sardis were.

From the acropolis one looks down on the dedicated valley of the Caicus which winds down to the Aegean Sea. Two streams, the Selinus and the Ketios, today cross the plain where the ancient city of Pergamum stood. Nowadays the site is entirely covered by the modern town—only the colossal Roman temple, dedicated to Serapis, towers above the houses around it.

The three principal sanctuaries of Asclepius were in Epidaurus, on the island of Cos (the sphere of Hippocrates' activities), and in Pergamum. The one in Pergamum was the biggest. The Emperors Caracalla and Marcus Aurelius refused to be medically treated anywhere except at the Asklepieion of Pergamum. Above its monumental entrance was the inscription: 'Death cannot enter the Asklepieion.' The reason for the universal belief of the ancient world that this spot had been specially chosen by the gods for the cure of all diseases was no doubt to be found in the numerous mineral springs of various chemical composition which well up in its vicinity. In Asia Minor the god of health was known not as Asclepius but as Telesphorus.

Pergamum's contribution to the artistic, cultural, and scientific advancement of mankind is of tremendous importance. There is, first of all, the earlier form of our paper which owes its name of parchment to the city of Pergamum and whose invention was no less important for human progress than that of the printing press. The Ptolemies in Alexandria and the Attalids in Pergamum founded the two famous museums of antiquity—a museum being a shrine of learning and the arts dedicated to the nine Muses. They were the first institutions in the world for the promotion of literature and historiography. In the second century B.C., when Ptolemy of Egypt realized that his rival Eumenes II was outstripping him in furnishing his great library in Pergamum, he prohibited the export of papyrus from Egypt. The result was that Pergamum began to experiment with the processing of hides as a writing material. A new method of tanning was developed which made it possible for both sides of the skin to be written on. The skins thus prepared were known as *pergamena*, which became our word parchment. The next invention was the reduced size of the 'sheet', which made it possible for these smaller sheets to be bound together into books which were a great deal easier to handle. Whereas a 'book' of 300 pages of papyrus would previously have filled about six leather buckets and required two men to carry it, such a book could now be carried in a man's pocket.

What other city on earth can claim that its name has become so closely linked with the intellectual advancement of the human race? Mark Antony made Cleopatra a present of 200,000 complete works from the library at Pergamum. By order of the Emperor Theodosius, Archbishop Theophilus of Alexandria later burnt that famous library because it contained only heathen works. This was one of the greatest tragedies in the history of the human mind.

Pergamum also had an important school of sculpture and painting. Archaic sculpture, which until then had been somewhat lifeless, first began to acquire more lively and dynamic traits in Pergamum. Here, too, the art of the mosaic was developed. In one of the city's gymnasia, painting and sculpture were taught for the first time in history and plays were performed by the pupils.

The city lies in that part of Aeolia which was then known as Mysia. Immediately south of the river Caicus the character of the landscape changes abruptly, becoming pastoral and Phrygian. The Phrygians had the reputation of being accomplished players on the flute. The high-pitched shrill tone of their flute, known as *elegn*, has given us the term elegy. Thus, at the very dawn of European music, thousands of years before Bach and Beethoven, sounds the plaintive tune of the Phrygian shepherd's pipe of ancient Anatolia.

Izmir

Half-way between Pergamum and Izmir the deep blue bay of Ali-Aga opens out behind Pitane. Here, on the seashore, once stood the city of Myrina, on the border of the land of the Amazons. In the *Iliad,* Myrina is the divine Queen of the Amazons, venerated by the Trojans as 'leaping Myrina'. Agamemnon, on his voyage to Troy, first dropped anchor in this port. Etymologically, Myrina means 'exalted life-giving mother'. Behind the Cape of Larissa, landlocked today, extends the valley of the Hermus with its green vineyards. This is where the familiar sultanas come from. The Hermus meanders right across the plain; in ancient times it formed the frontier between Aeolia in the north and Ionia in the south. The city of Izmir is an Amazon foundation. The Amazons are thought to have been the warlike priestesses of the Hittites: this view is supported by the fact that all round Izmir in the mountains Hittite sculptures have been found. The harbour is situated in one of the most beautiful bays of the entire Mediterranean and is one of its five greatest natural harbours. Its history goes back over several thousand years.

The city is laid out in the shape of a crescent along the slopes of a huge amphitheatre formed by high mountains which still bear the ruins of cyclopean acropolises of long-forgotten cities. High above the city centre towers the Pagus mountain with its circular citadel of Lysimachus, known as Kadife Kale. In the Bible it is referred to as 'the crown of the city'. From there one has a view over the entire Gulf, extending on both sides and at a distance of about fifty nautical miles opening out to the sea. Pagus means 'the region outside the city'. As the first Christians were townspeople, they referred to the inhabitants outside their city walls, who had not yet been converted, as *pagani*, which in consequence came to mean 'heathen'.

On the northern promontory of the gulf, hidden to view from the sea, lies the ancient port of Phocaea. Its ruins stand on two small bights directly by the sea. Ancient Phocaea was the first city of the Ionian League. Some of the Phocaeans migrated westward and founded Massalia (Marseilles), Nike (Nice), and Agde in the south of France, and thus brought Greek civilization to the barbarian Gauls. To the north of the gulf, east of the famous salt-lakes of Izmir, rise the heights of Sipylos, while in the north-east stood the ancient city of Smyrna, whose history goes back to mythological times when it played an important part in the Amazon kingdom.

Alyattes, king of Lydia and father of Croesus, conquered ancient Smyrna in the sixth century B.C. Until the arrival of Alexander the Great it became eclipsed and virtually ceased to exist. Today the place where it stood is called Bayrakli. Here, on a hill, was the tomb of Tantalus, to whom we owe the expression 'tantalizing'. As he had served to the gods the flesh of his own son, the punishment imposed on him was having to stand knee-deep in water in Hades, hungry and thirsty; whenever he bent down to quench his thirst the water would recede, and whenever he reached out for the fruits on the branch above him a gust of wind would blow the branch aside. Tantalus was the father of Pelops, who emigrated to Greece and gave his name to the Peloponnese. He was also the father of Atreus and thus the grandfather of Agamemnon and Menelaus. (These myths reflect pre-Achaean migrations from Anatolia to Greece.) Tantalus was also the father of Niobe, the Queen of Thebes in Greece.

Legend has it that Alexander the Great, while resting during a hunt, fell asleep on Mount Pagus. In his dream the goddess Nemesis appeared and announced to him that thrice blessed would be he who founded a new Smyrna on this bank of the river Meles. Alexander thereupon commanded his general Lysimachus to found the new city.

Alexander was also known to be a great admirer of Homer—and this, in fact, is Homer country. A well-known ancient epigram says: 'Seven cities are claiming Homer now he is dead—the seven cities where he begged for bread.' These seven cities, which claim the poet as their own, are Smyrna, Chios, Rhodes, Colophon, Salamis, Argos, and Athens. Four of these can certainly be ruled out as Homer's birthplace because the Ionian dialect was not spoken there. Now both the *Iliad* and the *Odyssey* contain a number of Aeolian expressions within the Ionian form of the language; but whereas in Colophon and Chios only Ionian was spoken, Smyrna, before becoming Ionian, had been part of Aeolia. This fact argues strongly in favour of Smyrna being Homer's birthplace. Moreover, the most important name given to the poet is Melesigenes, meaning 'the son of the river Meles', the river which flows through Izmir. It also shows that the part of the city west of the river—today the Meles runs right through the town—was not built until the time of Alexander the Great or even later.

On the far side of the bay stood the city of Clazomenae, the birthplace of the philosopher Anaxagoras, who founded the theory of the dualism of mind and matter. Opposite, at the foot of Mount Mimas, was a Minoan settlement. The mountain immediately east of Mount Pagus is called Olympus. There are altogether more than twenty mountains of that name in Anatolia. North of Mount Pagus, looking out on the Sipylos mountains beyond the bay, stood the ancient theatre of Smyrna. On this spot, in the Park of Culture, now stands a giant statue of Marcus Aurelius. A little to the west, in a hollow of the ground, was the ancient stadium where St. Polycarp suffered a martyr's death. To the south, behind the citadel, two crescent-shaped aqueducts cross the Meles which here roars down a ravine. In antiquity all these rivers and mountains were viewed as living things and personified.

Architectural and historical monuments are scattered throughout the city of Izmir. Karshi Yaka on the Sipylos coast was called Cordelio, a corruption of Cœur-de-Lion, Richard the Lionheart, who stopped here on a crusade. Ancient customs, even some from pre-classical times, have survived right through later religions and rites. The Turks, more particularly the Turkish women, are passionately attached to folk customs celebrating the beginning of spring. Tamuz was the god of deep water in ancient Sumer. Later he became Adonis, and in Anatolia Attis. On the first day of spring the Turkish women will assemble on the beach to this day and cast letters containing their wishes on to the water. One also sees a few young Turkish peasant girls with a single rose in their hair. The rose was the sacred flower of Aphrodite, and by wearing it a girl indicates that she is still unmarried. A good part of the ancient pagan past thus survives in the everyday life of the Muslim women of Asia Minor.

Ionia

This is a region of tobacco and fruit plantations. Naturally, the cities of Ephesus and Miletus are the most spectacular sites of Ionia, but the real, typical Ionia is the region of plains and valleys, a land of sun-scorched roads with the perfume of asphodels hanging on the air. In antiquity there were twelve Ionian cities, but Herodotus tells us that two of these, Ephesus and Colophon, were excluded from the Apaturia festivities 'because of a certain crime'. All of them, however, took part in the Panionian festivities in the sacred city of Panionium. This was situated on a promontory extending westward from the Mycale mountains to the island of Samos. Ephesus rises along the northerly slopes of these mountains, near the bay where the Cayster (Caistros) river runs into the sea.

History has seen three Ephesian capitals on the site of present-day Ephesus—the pre-Hellenistic, the Hellenistic, and the Byzantine cities. Each of these three epochs extended over several centuries. The first Ephesus, whose origins go right back to mythological times, stood on a hill overlooking the sea. It was said to have been founded by the Amazons around a shrine dedicated to Artemis. In the Hymn to Artemis by Callimachus are the lines: 'To thee the warlike Amazons erected an effigy under an oak tree at Ephesus by the sea, and Hippo made burnt offerings to thee, and they themselves first danced a war dance with shield and breastplate.' Callimachus concludes with the words: 'Let no one omit the annual dance.' Originally the site of the Temple was a *temenos*, a sacred grove. Later a niche in a tree-trunk sheltered the sacred image, a sacred boulder—probably a meteorite.

There are enough connections between the Hittites, who venerated a mother goddess, and the warlike women's kingdom of the Amazons to support the theory that the Hittite priestesses and their military victories provided the basis for the myths of the Amazons. Their capital was Themiscyra on the river Thermodon which flowed into the Black Sea. The place was near the centre of the Hittite sphere of power. Latest archaeological finds argue against an Ionian immigration and an encounter between Ionians and Carians. At the site of the first city of Ephesus a great many Mycenaean remains have been found, proving that Achaeans were settled there very much earlier than the eleventh century B.C., the putative date of the Ionian migration to Asia Minor. The first city of Ephesus and the city of Miletus, both of them south of the Mycale mountains, are entitled to be reckoned among the birthplaces of European civilization. This civilization may be said to have two roots—experimental science and the Christian religion. The Ionians were the first people on earth to free their thinking

74

from the fetters of religious ritual. They recognized no moralizing gods which circumscribed mankind with divine imperatives. Nor did they have any religious beliefs as far as life after death was concerned. To them the dead were insubstantial shadows. The Ionians took the view that the decay of the body meant the end of all its functions, and hence also thought. Death destroyed the human body, hence it also destroyed the ego. Freed from any hopes or fears connected with life after death, hopes or fears which might have restricted their thinking by preconceived ideas, the Ionians were free men who regarded the world around them as the only genuine reality. Slavery at that time had not yet reached the stage when a rich ruling caste or an oligarchy would despise all artistic, artisan, or technical activities. It was in Miletus that the human intellect first attempted to interpret the universe in purely materialistic terms. Thales of Miletus maintained that the sun and the moon were not deities but fiery bodies. To him the multiplicity and complexity of all observed phenomena was due to one universal, material element—water. All other substances he believed to originate from water by way of constant change. These then were the beginnings of the Miletan school of philosophy. One of its most brilliant exponents was Anaximander, who constructed the sundial and who postulated that the basis of the universe was an indefinite, unbounded substance which was not material but could change into material forms. Another thinker, Anaximenes, regarded the air as the basic substance of the universe and concluded that all other forms of matter were derived from it by way of condensation or rarefaction. The measure of the brilliance of these early philosophers is not in the answers they supplied to their questions but in the fact that they stopped to ask these questions at all.

Another philosopher of Miletus, Leucippus, put forward a new hypothesis about the physical basis of the universe. He postulated not a single substance but a multiplicity of substances. The Ionian thinkers did not call themselves philosophers but *physiologoi*—i.e., physicists in the modern meaning of the word. They believed that matter was eternal, yet at the same time alive.

Some time between 540 and 475 B.C. the greatest thinker of antiquity, Heraclitus, was born in the first city of Ephesus. Unlike his predecessors who believed in permanent material atoms, Heraclitus believed that the basis of the real world lay in a continuous change of material atoms. To him, being was the antithesis of non-being, and reality lay between being and non-being. He asserted that matter was in a constant state of change—*panta chorei* (everything is moving), *kai ouden menei* (and does not stop anywhere), *panta rhei* (everything is in flux). Democritus of Thrace, on the other hand, believed in the existence of a vast number of different compositions and compounds which produced the world as perceived by the senses.

To all these speculating natural philosophers, the *physiologoi*, the gods were no more than figments of primitive superstition. The Anatolian atomic theoreticians—starting with Thales but including also the dynamist Heraclitus—drove the deities from the earth, from the sea, from the stars, and from their life altogether, since they saw religion as an obstacle to intellectual adventure. For that reason these philosophers were branded atheists in the rest of Greece, where Athens was the centre of deism. Anaxagoras of Clazomenae, invited to Athens by his friend Pericles, was there sentenced to death because he declared that the sun and moon were not deities but material bodies.

This eruption of intellectual activity in Ionia is one of the most spectacular events in the history of mankind. Never before had anything comparable happened. But then it is perhaps hardly surprising that the country which produced Homer also became the cradle of science. The *physiologoi* were practical men concerned with the practical business of their cities; in the remainder of Greece a diametrically opposite view was held. There, philosophy became a purely theoretical contemplation of the world, strictly divorced from everyday life. There, contemplative thought was regarded as an essential means of enhancing the nobility of the human soul. This attitude went back to Orphic and Eleusinian influences, as personified in the Pythagorean principles. The Orphic teaching called for asceticism as a means of attaining mystic revela-

76

59 RHODES **Lindos with temple fortress**

60 RHODES Castle of the Knights of St. John and Turkish clock-tower

61
RHODES
Mosque of Suleiman
the Great with mina

62
CASTELORIZO
View from
an olive grove

63 CASTELORIZO Dawn over islands and sea

64 PYRGOS Stalactites in Glyphada caves

65
COS
Abandoned
rock dwellings

ASS
Troad coast faci
Lesb

71 HALICARNASSUS Castle of the Knights of St. John

72 PAMUKKALE Limestone sinter terraces of Hierapolis

tions, ecstasy, and thus union with the deity. Through Pythagoras these views reached Greece and were taken up by Plato. Whereas the Eleusinian mysteries and the Orphic cult were entirely focused on life after death, the Anatolian thinkers were wholly concerned with this world.

The Peloponnesian wars, from 431 to 404 B.C., led to a stagnation of philosophy in Asia Minor. The Ionian cities were compelled to throw in their lot with one or the other of the warring parties—either Sparta or Athens—as circumstances demanded. Each of these Greek powers tried to subject the Asia Minor cities economically, and they suffered grievously as a result.

Even before the outbreak of the war Athens attacked the island of Melos which lay outside its sphere of naval influence. The island surrendered in the face of such vastly superior power, and all boys and men of military age were executed; the remaining people were sold into slavery and the island was made a colony of Athens. The Spartans were no more humane in their treatment of the cities they beleaguered. The inhabitants of Platea, for instance, were starved out to such a degree that they were reduced to eating human flesh. When they finally surrendered to the besieging forces they were slaughtered and their city razed to the ground. The Anatolian cities which joined the Athenian League were in effect no more than satellites under an Athenian yoke. Thus Athens sentenced the entire population of Lesbos to death, and only suspended the carrying out of the sentence for reasons of political expediency. It did, however, confiscate the Lesbian fleet and parcelled up the island into 3000 plots which were leased to Athenian citizens. True enough, the plots were cultivated by inhabitants of Lesbos but they had to pay an excessively high ground rent to their Athenian absentee landlords.

Ephesus

Even a short note on Ephesus must contain a few remarks about its different historical periods, its changing political systems, its philosophy, and its aesthetics. The earliest Ephesus was already famous for its Temple of Artemis, one of the Seven Wonders of the World. This was four times the size of the Parthenon in Athens and was regarded as the model for all temples in the Ionian style, the style which in antiquity itself was regarded as classical—*i.e.*, perfect. Whereas the Corinthian style begins to strike us as over-rich and a little decadent, the Ionian style is a perfect expression of the creative and inventive Ionian spirit. The plan for the Temple of Artemis was drawn up by Chersiphron of Cnossus and his son Metagenes, while its construction, which took 200 years, was chiefly in the hands of two Ephesians by the name of Peonius and Demetrius.

This temple may well be described as the first banking institution in the world. It owned valuable tracts of land, quarries, fishing rights, and pastures in the region of the Cayster valley. It possessed an exceptional wealth of temple treasure and operated on an annual budget. It was the richest deposit bank of the ancient world; it lent sums of money against notes of hand, and it issued letters of credit. The wealthy entrusted their money and valuables to the temple for safe-keeping, because the right of asylum enjoyed by the holy places assured them of complete security. The temple was a bank for the whole of the ancient Orient and had an international character. According to tradition it was set on fire by a madman, one Herostratus. The building contained 127 columns over sixty-five feet high and—with the exception of the door and a few roof-beams, as well as two narrow flights of stairs—was entirely built of stone. A mounted unit of men, who rode around it continuously, guarded the Temple of Artemis by night and day. Inside, in addition to about two hundred priests, there were further guards. It therefore appears exceedingly unlikely that an edifice so substantially built and so closely guarded could have been set on fire by a single person.

The Turks, just by way of illustration, had large quantities of gunpowder stored in the Parthenon and the Venetians bombarded it with incendiary shells and eventually detonated it—yet the major part of that temple stands to this day. And the Temple of Ephesus was four times the size of the Parthenon! It seems much more likely that the priests themselves first robbed the temple and subsequently, to cover up their theft, set it on fire, and then put the blame on a lunatic who could not defend himself. There have been many other instances in history when such doubtful hypotheses were passed on from one generation to the next as historical truths.

The temple was finally destroyed by the Archbishop of Constantinople. In the sixth century A.D. the Emperor Justinian used it as a quarry for his own Byzantine buildings in Constantinople.

The festivities in honour of the goddess Artemis, which consisted of the mysteries and the festivities proper, took up a whole month each year. The mysteries were held throughout two or three days in spring. A procession of pilgrims left the city by the Magnesia Gate to climb the sacred Mount Solmissos, which contained the sacred cave of Ortygia. Under the trees in the cool, sacred grove by the bank of the babbling Cenchryos stream the solemn sacrifices were made. This spot is now known as Panayia Kapulu and, according to Catholic tradition, the Virgin Mary spent the last years of her life there.

Tacitus says in his Annals that in Asia Minor there was such an abundance of sacred sites, where culprits could find asylum, that temporal justice was totally unable to apprehend them. In order to remedy this state of affairs all sanctuaries were ordered to send representatives to Rome to prove the authenticity of their sacred places.

During the thirty days of festivities in honour of the goddess everybody in Ephesus was enjoined to be merry 'without desecrating a single day by work of any kind'. The statue of Artemis, because of the goddess's close connection with the sea, was carried down to the shore, washed, and symbolically fed with salt from the sea. Taking part in these festivities were the high priests, known as the Megabyzes, the virgins of the city, the innumerable servants of the goddess, priests, priestesses, sacred heralds, trumpeters, sceptre-bearers, theologians, the mounted temple guard, the robing women of the goddess, acrobats, mountebanks, and flute players.

For its time the Temple of Artemis was a building in an entirely revolutionary style. Until then the primitive Doric style had been prevalent; in Ephesus the new Ionian style, the prototype of the style that was to become the classical manner, was created and developed to the peak of perfection.

Another architectural monument, equally outstanding in its own way, was built in the sixth century A.D. by Justinian (for whom the Hagia Sophia was being built at the same time)—the Basilica of St. John, a huge building on a cruciform plan, with four domes along the bars of the cross and one each over the aisles, which were supported by four powerful columns. The tomb of St. John is at the intersection of the bars of the cross.

Theologians are still not quite certain whether St. John the Evangelist and St. John the Divine were two people or one and the same person. Today the balance of opinion is increasingly swinging towards the latter view, chiefly because the first seven churches of Asia Minor are mentioned in Revelations. On the other hand, the fact that the style of Revelations differs so entirely from that of the Gospel would seem to argue in favour of separate authors. It is, however, quite feasible that St. John the Evangelist came to Ephesus in his youth—if he ever went there at all—and subsequently lived to a ripe old age; on this assumption, the style of Revelations could be explained as that of an old man. If we accept this explanation, then the tomb in Ephesus is that of St. John the Evangelist as well as St. John the Divine. Among many other archaeological remains those worth particular mention include the Byzantine gate of the ancient city wall and, situated on a hill, the Turkish Seljuk fortress with its towers.

From an early date in antiquity forest fires were deliberately started with a view to gaining land for agriculture and pasturage. This has led to the denudation of the mountains, from which the winter rains washed all the top soil down to the coast, completely ruining the land. In the interior the dry seasons caused further erosion, resulting in famines, while at the same time the natural harbours were turned into malarial swamps. Hunger and malaria were undoubtedly major factors in the decline of the Ionian civilization. The forests took their revenge for their despoliation.

The inhabitants of ancient Ephesus believed malaria to be a plague sent by the gods, and therefore made sacrifices to them to gain their favour. When the sacrifices remained unheard the locality came to be regarded as cursed by the gods. At the time of Lysimachus, therefore, a second city was founded at some distance from the first. This new city, the Hellenistic Ephesus, was built on two hills and on the broad mountain, Coressus, immediately west of Mount Pion. The wall of Lysimachus extended across the ridge of Mount Coressus over a length of almost six miles. About the same time the harbour of Ephesus became silted up and the sea retreated. The Christian era began. In the meantime the swamps of the first Ephesus had dried out and thus a third city, the Byzantine city, could now be built on the site of the first. The Basilica of St. John, the Mosque of Isa Bey, the Byzantine city gate, and the fortress on the hill belong to this period.

Among the remains of the Hellenistic city—the second city of Ephesus—two are of particular interest. The first of these is the so-called Cave of the Seven Sleepers. Seven Christians, while being pursued, took refuge in a cave where they hid out and were immured by their pursuers. They fell asleep under the reign of the Emperor Decius and did not wake up until 200 years later, under the Emperor Theodosius; they believed that they had been asleep for only one night. They told their story and died. Now the cave is a kind of honeycomb of thousands of graves, arranged in layers on top of each other. Three churches have been built inside it. The oldest Christian monument is the Orthodox Synaxar, a calendar of saints. This mentions that Mary Magdalen died in Ephesus and was buried in this cave. In point of fact, her name has been found on a burial niche deep in the cave. It is possible that this tomb of Mary Magdalen caused the cave to be regarded as a sacred place and subsequently gave rise to the legend of the Seven Sleepers. In view of the documentary evidence of Mary Magdalen's presence at this place, the Virgin Mary must also be assumed to have stayed there. But whereas the Orthodox Church accepts St. Mary Magdalen's stay in Ephesus, it is convinced that the Virgin Mary died at Gethsemane in the Holy Land. The Roman Catholic Church, as already noticed, supports the opposite view.

Ephesus had several large gymnasia, of which the eastern or girls' gymnasium is the most important. Since the civilization of Asia Minor sprang from matriarchal origins the women there received a better education than elsewhere. Thus the most highly educated women of antiquity all came from Anatolia—Artemisia, the young Queen of Halicarnassus, the ally of Xerxes, who personally commanded her fleet in the battle of Salamis; Aspasia of Miletus, whose house Pericles would never leave without twice embracing her, who participated in the forty-nine conversations of Socrates and Plato, and whom Pericles was given special permission by the Council of Athens to marry—a great exception since Athenians were normally only permitted to marry Athenian women; Archeanassa of Colophon, who was loved by Plato; and the immortal Sappho of Lesbos.

The second city of Ephesus is a city of ruins unparalleled in the world. It is the only place that conveys a clear picture of what an ancient city, a great cultural centre, was really like. The snow-white, marble-paved roads are spotlessly clean, thanks to a highly competent sewerage system which could bear comparison with that of many a modern town. The stadia hold memories of athletic contests and cheering crowds, and the huge agoras, the market-places, bring back the babel of the voices of merchants. To this day one can see women drawing water from the wells—graceful, carrying large amphoras on their heads as in ancient times, gossiping about their husbands while the water spills over on the flagstones.

We can still see the enormous bath-houses, like that of Scholastica, where rich foreign traders were invited to drink wine with sensuous, dancing slave girls and where, when they moved off a fortnight later, an appropriate bill would be presented to them. There is an elegant odeum, where the notes of lyres and shrill flutes resounded, and the library of the proconsul Celsius, where scholars would search the ancient papyri for any lost gems of science. There were the temples, where incense would be burnt by the faithful kneeling in mystic surrender before the altar of the god Serapis, and the brothels, where the visitors were first made to take off their sandals, wash their feet and pray to Aphrodite.

There is also the Church of Our Lady, where in A.D. 431 the Council of Ephesus assembled in order to define the attributes of the Holy Virgin and where the Archbishop of Alexandria hurled his anathema at Nestorius, the Archbishop of Constantinople. Nestorius was excommunicated by the Council as a heretic, and after much argument Jesus Christ was declared the Son of God. Down the wide Arcadian Way, lined by hundreds of statues on each side, Mark Antony, arrayed as Bacchus, once drove in an open carriage with Cleopatra. They were cheered by all Ephesus, dressed up for the occasion as fauns, Maenads and the other mythological companions of the god of wine. Down the same Arcadian Way, right to the edge of the sea, walked Scipio Africanus, the disillusioned general, accompanied by his friend, the poet Terence.

Here, too, strolled Petronius Arbiter during his term as proconsul; here Hannibal lived for a while; here Mithridates, the King of Pontus, entered the city drunk with victory, having slain 80,000 Romans. To list the names of the kings, emperors, poets, philosophers, and artists who came to Ephesus would fill a hundred pages. We shall mention only Archilochus, Mimnermus of Colophon, Apelles of Colophon, Phocylides of Miletus, Callinus, Hipponax of Ephesus, Antimachus, Xenophon, and Parhassius.

The history of Ephesus is a record of countless changes of fortune, a continuous coming and going of conquerors—the Cimmerii, then Croesus, under whose protection the city enjoyed a period of prosperity; then Cyrus, the King of Persia. The Athenians encouraged the Ionians to rise against Persian rule, but after their defeat deserted them. Later they came back, together with the Spartans, this time as conquerors. Once more the Persians overran the country, followed by Alexander the Great who believed that all political problems could be solved with the sword, just as he had cut the Gordian Knot. After his short life he was deified, while his generals were turning Asia Minor into a battlefield. Lysimachus fought against the Seleucids, Antiochus arrived, Antigonus departed. The Pergamese came and went. The Romans stood at the gates. *Sic transit gloria mundi.*

We have dealt with Ephesus in detail because, in a manner of speaking, it illustrates the whole of classical civilization. It was here that the peninsula of Asia Minor, present-day Turkey, first reached its ethnic and political unity seven centuries ago. South of the Mycale mountains stretches the plain of the Maeander. To the right the land is flat all the way to the skyline, but in the south rises the Latma range like a wall. Mount Latma itself, according to mythology, is the home of Endymion. Right across this plain the Maeander slowly winds its course to the sea. When in spate it carries with it vast amounts of soil. In antiquity the landowners whose soil was thus washed away by the river could sue the river in the courts of Miletus, whereupon a fine was imposed on it and the damage made good from the proceeds derived from river tolls and rights. Year after year such actions were laid against it. Miletus, the city which once had six harbours, lies on the southern bank of the Maeander. Twelve miles south of the city stands the huge Temple of Apollo of Didyma. On the southern flank of the Mycale range, in the direction of the promontory jutting out westward into the sea, lies the little town of Priene.

Halicarnassus

Halicarnassus, the present-day Bodrum, was originally a Carian city on the south-western coast of Asia Minor. In the most ancient period it extended only over the peninsula of Zephyria, so named because of the eternal spring which seemed to reign there. In ancient mythology Zephyrus, the god of spring and the winds, breathed life into Chloris, the flower nymph, and she gave birth to Carpus, the god of fruits. Today the peninsula of Zephyria is the site of the huge fortress of the Knights of St. John, a fortress dedicated to St. Peter and therefore called Petronium which became the Turkish Bodrum. The ancient name of the city, Halicarnassus, goes back to a lost language of Asia Minor. In historical times it spread westward and embraced Salamakis, a city of the Carians and Leleges. At a later date the Dorians arrived from Troezen and Argos, a city founded by the legendary Antaeus, the son of the earth goddess Gaea (Ge), who had been cast down to earth by Zeus after the battle of the Titans and was able to regain new strength from every contact with his mother earth. The Dorians therefore took pride in calling themselves Antaeads, the progeny of Antaeus. In early historical times Halicarnassus was a member of the Dorian Hexapolis, an alliance of six cities, whose other members were Cos, Cnidus, Lindus, Camirus, and Ialysus. It was the custom in the games held in honour of Apollo at Cnidus for the victors to leave their trophies to the temple. When a citizen of Halicarnassus, by name of Agasicles, won the prize but decided to keep it for himself, his city was expelled from the alliance. However, Halicarnassus by then had so far outstripped the other members of the alliance in greatness and commercial power that the incident at Cnidus was probably only a pretext for its exclusion. Following Lydian rule, Halicarnassus for a while became a vassal of Athens and had to pay tribute to it. About 480 B.C. Herodotus was born at Halicarnassus. In the same year Artemisia, the daughter of Lygdamis, the beautiful young Queen of Halicarnassus, commanded her own fleet in the battle of Salamis, as an ally of Xerxes.

Herodotus says: 'I greatly admire Artemisia, for although she was but a woman yet she waged war against the Greeks; because her husband had died she held the reins of power in her own hands... She went to war herself with courage and spirit of adventure, although she need not have done so.' On the eve of the battle she is recorded as having said to Xerxes: 'See to your ships and do not venture to engage in battle at sea, for their men are as much superior to yours at sea as men are superior to women.' And Herodotus also reports: 'The captains of the Athenian galleys were then commanded ... and a reward of 10,000 drachmai was promised to him who would take her prisoner alive.' The Athenians considered it shameful to be fighting a woman.

After Artemisia's death her son Pisinadalis succeeded to the throne, and he in turn was followed by Hecatomnus from an ancient dynasty of Mylas. In 377 B.C. Hecatomnus' son Mausolus became King of Halicarnassus. Since Xerxes had allowed some of the tyrants to continue to rule their cities, Mausolus could be said to have in fact been one of his satraps. He made Halicarnassus his capital, because of its favourable strategic and fine geographical situation, and incorporated in it the population of six more cities in the region of Pedasis. Under his rule the city reached its highest peak of prosperity. Mausolus endeavoured to subject also the neighbouring islands and supported the islands of Rhodes, Cos, and Chios in their rebellion against Athens. In 357 B.C. his policy succeeded and Caria became one of the principal naval powers in the Aegean. After his death, in 353 B.C., he was succeeded by his wife Artemisia II, who was also his sister, and who destroyed the fleet of Rhodes when that island attempted to secede after the death of her brother-husband. She conquered the entire island and proved a worthy successor of Artemisia I and a highly competent queen of a sea-faring country.

The Mausoleum of Halicarnassus, one of the Seven Wonders of the World of antiquity, was begun by Artemisia II in memory of her husband Mausolus. When she died in 351 B.C. she was followed by her brother Idrieus, who reigned for seven years. After his death his wife and co-regent Ada was exiled to Alinda by Pixidorus and there, in 334 B.C., concluded an alliance with Alexander the Great against Halicarnassus. A siege followed. The chief satrap, Memnon, who commanded the Persian fleet, had ordered a deep moat to be dug all round the walls. The city was defended with outstanding bravery against the Macedonian battle-chariots, cavalry, and infantry phalanx. When Alexander had gained possession of the external walls and the citadel of Salamakis still refused to surrender, he gave orders for it to be destroyed and the citizens to be shared out among the surrounding villages. Queen Ada was reinstated as ruler of the city.

After her death she was succeeded by Asandus, Antigonus (in 313 B.C.), Lysimachus, Philip V of Macedonia (in 201 B.C.), Ptolemy Epiphanes, and eventually, in 190 B.C., by the Romans. Although Ptolemy had a gymnasium built, as well as a 'stoa' and porticus, the city never in fact recovered from the great siege, and Cicero describes it as virtually abandoned. In 129 B.C. Halicarnassus and the whole of Caria became part of the Roman province of Asia and thus came directly under Roman rule. This state of affairs continued throughout the entire Roman and Byzantine epochs.

In the eleventh century Halicarnassus was occupied for a short while by the Turkish Seljuks, but was soon reconquered by the Byzantines. In the thirteenth century it fell into the hands of the Beys of Menteshé, and under the rule of Bayazid I was incorporated in the Ottoman Empire. When that empire was destroyed by Tamerlane in the battle of Ankara in 1402, the Knights of St. John of the Cross, then settled in Rhodes, took possession of the undefended city. They began to build a fortified castle on the Zephyria peninsula, at the very spot where the acropolis of the ancient Doric city had stood. Construction went on for ninety-eight years. When Suleiman II conquered Rhodes, the Knights of St. John fled also from Halicarnassus and left their powerful castle behind—unscathed but empty. It suffered some damage in the First World War, but most of it is well-preserved and is now used as a museum.

The medieval castle of the Knights of St. John is an exceptionally massive fortress with complicated defences consisting of casemates, ramparts, walls, scarps, and fortified counter-scarps, glacis, outer defences with fortified towers and intervening court-yards. It forms a gigantic labyrinth of passages, linked together by bridges, protec-ted by towers and surrounded by moats. Since it covers the whole of the Zephyria peninsula it appears to rise straight from the sea. The walls are covered with the coat of arms of the Knights of St. John, and also with prayers carved into the stonework, especially around 1500 when the Ottoman Turks were approaching the city. The architectural style of the various towers reflects the different European styles of forti-fication architecture—because each nationality among the Knights built its own tower.

The fortress is one of the finest of its kind, a true jewel in the Mediterranean. Con-struction began in 1415 and was completed in 1513. But a mere ten years later, in 1523, the fortress was abandoned. The museum it now houses contains rare pieces of Mycenaean pottery and is unique. The sea-floor around Halicarnassus abounds in jagged reefs which have claimed a great many ships over the centuries and hence represent a veritable submarine museum. At present the American Geographic Society, several American universities and a number of diving clubs are busily en-gaged in raising its treasures from the sea-floor and setting them up in the museum.

Halicarnassus, as we have said, was the site of one of the Seven Wonders of the an-cient world—the monumental tomb of King Mausolus which has given to our voca-bulary the term mausoleum. It consisted of four tiers—the ground floor or podium, an Ionian colonnade and walls, then a pyramid, and finally a group of horses with chariot, the quadriga. In spite of all their feeling for balance and proportion, the architects were bold enough to place four monuments of different style one on top of another. To erect a pyramid on top of slender columns and walls was an architectural tour-de-force which amazed the world. But then Asia Minor has always been a land of new ideas. In A.D. 1402, although the quadriga and the upper part of the pyramid had collapsed as a result of earthquakes, the Mausoleum was still in a comparatively good state of preservation. But when the Knights of St. John arrived they tore the

88

building down, used the marble statues for lime-making, and dragged away the blocks of marble in order to use them as building stones. Quite recently two fragments of a frieze were saved from a wall and these are now in the castle museum.

Hardly anything survives of ancient Halicarnassus. All that is preserved are a few sections of the city wall, a few catacombs hewn into the rock, and the remains of the eastern city gate; everything else lies below the surface. In 1875 Newton found a few friezes and took them to London to the British Museum.

The castle of St. Peter—as the fortress of the Knights of St. John is called—divides the harbour into two crescent-shaped bays which open towards the deep blue Mediterranean. At the western end was the site of the cult of Salamakis or Hermaphroditus. Both twin harbours are lined by houses painted brilliant white, with palms, eucalyptus trees, and shrubs providing splashes of rich green between them. Above the city rises the fortress, and all along the foreshore the colourful fishing-boats ride at anchor.

The surroundings of Bodrum are not only historically interesting, but also of exceptional scenic beauty. Magnificent wild regions alternate with idyllic ones. At night the bright stars look down on a scene which seems to belong to a different world. The coastline along the whole gulf is of truly magic beauty: breath-taking in its grandeur and completely untouched. In some places the cliffs rise to some thousand feet above the sea, elsewhere the coast is intersected by the estuaries of small rivers and bays, crumbled cities, walls, towers, temples, and bathing beaches, behind which extends the majestic backcloth of the mountains.

From Priene another road leads straight to the east, past the ancient cities of Tralles (Aydin) and Nisa (Sultan Hissar) to Hierapolis (Pamukkale) and Laodicea. This sector of road may be described as Phrygian; the scenery here is totally different from the south coast of Asia Minor. Most of the nomads use this road when they move from their summer quarters to their winter ones in spring and move back in autumn. Sometimes camel caravans two or three miles long are encountered here. Invariably riding on the lead camel is the most beautiful girl of the tribe, because her beauty is said to bring luck to the caravan. A Turkish proverb says that it is better to carry heavy stones with a beautiful woman than to eat honey with an ugly one.

Hierapolis

At Denizli on the northern side of the Maeander valley a huge white rock juts out from the mountain-slope, and on its summit, in a magnificent position looking far out over the land, stands the ruined city of Hierapolis. On the opposite flank of the valley rise the dark blue rocks and the blindingly white snowfields of the Cadmus mountains. Behind the ruins, the sun-parched mountains of Phrygia, cleft here and there by wooded ravines, melt their rose-tinted peaks into the blue of the sky. In front, the terrace drops steeply towards the arid, treeless desert of the Licusta valley. Hot springs have been spilling over the edge of the projecting rock for thousands of years, leaving behind a substance of white frothy limestone which makes the whole scene look like a huge cascading river suddenly turned to stone. A cascade of petri-fied foam, above which the vapours of the hot springs hang like a veil—a flight of fancy turned reality. In a few places the hot springs have produced conical shapes like champagne glasses. The scenery is gigantic and monstrous at the same time—an un-earthly scene, a setting for titans or for a witches' sabbath, weird and magnificent.

All this is the work of the hot springs which rise in a small lake called Plutonium. Its water is emerald green and perfectly transparent. In antiquity a marble colonnade, presumably of Ionian columns, surrounded the pool; it was later destroyed in an earthquake. The fragments of the columns littering the bed of the lake look like a water-nymph's fairy-tale palace, surrounded by brilliant red oleander bushes. The hot water which has been flowing down over the centuries has covered the entire low-lying land with a white encrustation. The water has been used for the dyeing of wool

90

since time immemorial. It is on these hot springs, and on their curative effects, that the reputation of Hierapolis was founded.

The sacred city—for that is what its name means—was probably founded by the Kings of Pergamum in the second century B.C. But it must have been known as a health-restoring spot and inhabited at a much earlier date. Later the city came under Roman rule, later still it was destroyed by an earthquake. It was subsequently rebuilt, and in the second and third centuries A.D. reached its heyday. Here, numerous Jews were converted to Christianity, and here at Hierapolis St. Philip suffered a martyr's death in A.D. 80. The impressive ruins take up the whole terrace of the projecting rock. A road lined by colonnades runs from a south-eastern gate right across the city in a north-westerly direction. On its left lies the agora, on its right lie the ruins of a small church; higher up on the hillside is a large Roman theatre. On a slope opposite, to the north, is the Shrine of the Martyrdom of St. Philip, an example of the earliest Byzantine architecture. By Lake Plutonium are the remains of a nymphaeum. Continuing along this colonnade-lined road, we come to two more churches—one of them small, the other enormous and dedicated to St. Philip. The area occupied by the city's cemeteries is more than twice that occupied by the city itself, so that one is justified in speaking of a necropolis, a city of the dead. Here are graves of every kind: sarcophagi, tumuli, and—a type peculiar to Hierapolis—the cradle-graves, in which the dead rest in a covered cradle supported on a plinth. The tumuli are in the northern necropolis; on top of each conical mound is a gravestone in the shape of a phallus. Hierapolis was also the birthplace of Epictetus (A.D. 60–140), the great Stoic philosopher who started life as a slave of Epaphroditus, the secretary of the Emperor Nero. In antiquity, according to tradition, there was also a cave here which emitted poisonous gases so that birds passing overhead dropped down dead. It was known as Charon's cave. To this day, visitors are shown a spot which the local peasants have surrounded with large boulders so that their livestock should not approach it and die—evidently Charon's cave, now filled up with stones and debris.

Lycia

The western boundary of Lycia lies a little to the east of Marmaris in south-western Asia Minor. In the east it borders on Pamphylia, the region of snow-covered Mount Solyma, and other peaks of the Taurus range.

The ancient authors regarded the Lycians as Creto-Carians. Their script has not yet been deciphered. Herodotus says of them: 'This one custom they alone practise, and no other nation—that they call their names after their mothers and not after their fathers.' That is, the ancient Lycians had a matriarchal order of society, a system typical of ancient Anatolia. The mythical poet Olev is said to have invented the hexameter in honour of Apollo and to have brought it to Delos. In the *Iliad* the Lycians are mentioned as loyal allies of the Trojans; Glaucus, a Lycian, led his fellow-countrymen into battle, and Pandareus and gallant Sarpedon likewise fought in the Trojan war. Their gallantry was immortalized by Horace and Ovid.

A particularly characteristic feature of their civilization are the graves hewn into the rock face. West of Marmaris, just under a couple of miles from the seashore, stands the first city of Caunus (Dalyan), with its acropolis behind a swampy plain. The Lycian pilasters and gables of its tombs can be seen on the sheer rock faces a great distance away. Farther north lies Cibyra, also with a necropolis, a theatre and other ruins. Then comes Halynda, another city of graves, amidst the sweet smell of wild thyme.

The biggest city in Lycia was Telmessus (Fethiye). It is surrounded by sheer rock faces which, along a blue circular bay, seem to rise up to the clouds. Like honeycombs, these cliffs are riddled with tombs hewn straight out of the rock, tombs as big as entire temples, with Ionian pilasters, gables and whole façades. The Xanthus, the namesake of the river in Troy, flows right across Lycia. On its banks lie cities whose very names suggest the ancient guitar and flute—Kemer, Tlos (Duver), Xanthus (Kinik), and Patara. The city of Xanthus also has a necropolis with tombs of four dif-

92

77
ANATOLIA
Artesian well
in the steppe

78
BELKIS
Old Seljuk bridge

79
MANAVGAT
Last rapids
before
the sea

80
ALANYA
Harbour,
jetty
and Red Tower

81 ANTALYA   Mosque of Ala ud-Din Kaikobad
82 ANAMUR KALESI   Corsair fortress facing Cyprus

83 SIDE   Theatre of the Fourteen Thousand

84 MYRA Ancient Lycian rock tombs with dressed-stone façades

ferent types, and on its acropolis there is a stele with a Lycian inscription which has not yet been deciphered.

The inhabitants of ancient Xanthus already had a political system based on proportional representation. A peaceful people, they founded a league even before Alexander the Great, and this league survived into the Roman epoch, until A.D. 43. Patara is regarded as the birthplace of Apollo and of St. Nicholas. The big rollers which arrive here from the African coast and break as they strike the beach have piled up the alluvial sand of the river into a massive bank so that the estuary is no longer visible from the sea. On a calm day the steep forest-clad mountains around the bay are reflected in the mirror-smooth water. After his defeat in Italy, Hannibal commanded an Antiochian fleet and, until the battle of Myonnesus, would sail up and down these coasts. St. Paul the Apostle also passed along here on his journey. Lycian settlements of lesser importance are Antiphellus (Kash) and Polenus, as well as Tristomon with a long line of tombs running down the rocky coast. Here we encounter the true type of the classical Lycian tomb—not hewn into the rock face, but each placed on a huge block of stone. Basically, their shapes echo the forms of the wooden dwellings and barns of the ancient Lycians. Opposite the island of Dolichiste (Kekova) is the charming little town of Aperlae with a rock theatre. The mountain ranges here run parallel to the coast, one behind another, in ever paler hues of blue.

After Andriace we come to Myra (Demre), made famous by St. Nicholas who was bishop there and also died there. In the tenth century the merchants of Bari and Venice competed for the possession of his relics, and since Bari moved faster than Venice, the Venetians had to content themselves with the bones of an uncle of the Saint. Myra, too, is situated on a hill with a whole series of Lycian tombs.

We next come to Cape Chelidonia, the 'Cape of Swallows'; its rocky cliffs of nearly 3500 feet make it the second highest cape in Asia Minor, second only to that of Kiran on the Ceramic Gulf. Five small rocky islands, devoid of all vegetation, which lie off it (they are the peaks of a submerged spur), are a favourite resting-place for the swallows returning from Africa. The strong southerly winds represent a constant danger to all small ships, and many of them are wrecked on these rocks every year. The city of Olympus is the last on the Lycian coast. Beyond it, to the east, we are already in Pamphylia, whose snow-capped mountain tops, as magnificent as any Alpine peaks, can be seen a long way off from out at sea, towering behind countless lesser ranges. Here rises Mount Solyma, a peak reached by a long scramble through scattered boulders, oleander bushes, and herds of goats. Here, according to legend, Bellerophon, mounted on Pegasus, slew the Chimaera, a fire-belching monster with the head of a lion, the body of a goat, and the tail of a serpent. All that is left of the monster is its fiery tongue—a flame flickering from a cleft in the rock to this day. Near the flame are the ruins of a Temple of Hephaestus.

Pamphylia

At a height of over 3000 feet, like an eagle's nest, the city of Termessus stands on top of the Mount of Roses, so-called because of the vast number of wild roses which cover its slopes in springtime. These slopes are so steep that the city is accessible only on foot or horseback. For that reason, probably, Termessus was the only fortified city which Alexander the Great in the course of his many campaigns besieged without capturing; the ancient historians report him to have suffered extraordinary losses in the course of that siege and to have exclaimed: 'There is a long way to go yet; I cannot spend my entire strength here.' The city had a large forum and a necropolis with beautifully carved sarcophagi, but not in the Lycian style. At the edge of the precipice lies the theatre from where a magnificent panorama opens up across the mountain ranges and the vast plain of Pamphylia.

Antalya was founded by King Attalus II of Pergamum and named after him. It is situated in a well-watered part of the otherwise very arid peninsula of Asia Minor.

Some twenty-five springs originate on the plateau of the Taurus mountains and these spill into the plain through narrow ravines as bigger or lesser streams carrying brilliantly clear water. The biggest four are called Esen, Aksu, Koprusugu, and Manavgat. The most turbulent of them, the Aksu, rushes down from the mountains with a deafening roar reminiscent of the frenetic music of cymbals and drums produced by the ancient priestesses of Cybele. On reaching the plain, the river becomes calmer and continues peacefully between oleanders down to the coast where it falls into the sea in several cascades.

There are cascades everywhere: thirteen of them alone fall from the rocky terraces of the city of Antalya, and some ten miles farther east enormous quantities of water fall straight into the sea from a height of 200 feet. But most of the rivers of the region vanish in black precipices and do not re-emerge until about twelve miles farther on. Such subterreanean river courses are known as *dudes*.

Viewed from the sea, the plain of Pamphylia, the 'land of all tribes', resembles a flat green ocean whose waves rise higher and higher the farther one goes inland, until they break in the spume-white summits of the distant snow-capped Taurus mountains. The perfume which hangs over the plain defies description—bitter lavender, the pungent smell of wild thyme and origan, and the heavy breath of orange blossom, jasmine, and myrtle fill the air and are wafted by the wind as far as Cilicia.

In ancient Pamphylia there were five important cities—Antalya, Perge, Sillium, Aspendos, and Side. The remains of the town wall of Antalya stand to this day among the little houses on the rocky cliffs which surround the deep blue bay. This is the only site in Pamphylia which has been continually inhabited through the centuries. It has spread beyond the old walls into the green of lemon, orange, and grapefruit. In the city centre stands an ancient Byzantine church which today serves as a museum; next to it is a slender blue minaret and not far away stands a triumphal arch dedicated to the Emperor Hadrian; this subsequently had two towers built on to it and was turned into the city gate. Everywhere we find Byzantine churches, Turkish mosques, caravanserais with bath-houses and libraries dating back to the Pergamese, Roman, Byzantine, and Seljuk periods.

East of the city lie the ruins of Perge, which was situated on a road running from east to west, and was moreover linked to the sea by the river Cestrus which was still navigable in antiquity. To begin with, it consisted only of the acropolis, then it spread southward into the plain, and in the course of the centuries once more retreated up to the acropolis where it gradually declined. Among the white marble ruins there still rises the theatre and a huge stadium with accommodation for 15,000 spectators. The vaults underneath the rows of seats were used as shops. The long main street of Perge, lined by colonnades and statues, exceeds many a modern town centre in splendour and beauty of proportion. St. Paul and Barnabas made their landfalls here on their journeys to Asia Minor.

Farther east the sapphire-blue Manavgat, a river exceedingly rich in rainbow trout, rushes past the village of the same name, down to the sea. Farther still to the east flows the Eurymedon, which was navigable as far as Aspendos in antiquity. Here the piers of a Roman bridge can still be seen, whereas the present bridge, a magnificent piece of architecture, dates back to the Seljuk era.

Aspendos stood on the flat brow of a hill and, in Roman times, extended far down over a second hill of lesser height. The site is a mass of ruins of ancient agoras, a small odeum, basilicas, an impressive aqueduct, and a stadium. The most striking building is the Roman amphitheatre, the best preserved of its kind. Altogether the Roman architecture of Anatolia is characterized by a particularly happy sense of balance, achieved to a degree not encountered elsewhere. The proscenium of the theatre rises to seven tiers, and the horseshoe auditorium consists of forty rows of seats which are in a good state of preservation.

The biggest city of Pamphylia was Side, more than 500 years older than Antalya. It was an important harbour on the trade route from Antioch to the West, a foundation of the Aeolians of Cyme in 750 B.C. In its market several thousands of slaves were sold by auction every day. Side also has the most impressive theatre in Anatolia, a forum with exceptionally large arcades, several aqueducts, temples, Byzantine walls, a Byzantine church and an arsenal. Famous figures who have visited this city include Alexander the Great, Mithridates, Julius Caesar, Pompey, Mark Antony, and Cleopatra.

Alanya, situated on what is already the Cilician coast, was at one time the winter residence of the Seljuk rulers. Later it became a pirate stronghold and had to be flushed out by Pompey in the last pre-Christian century during his war against Mithridates. The Seljuks settled in the ancient Coracesium, where Ala ud-Din Kaikobad built a castle. Near its monumental octagonal tower lies the arsenal, where five large galleys could be built simultaneously. The castle wall, which climbs up the rock, fits harmoniously into the landscape. High up on the cliffs stand the typical timber houses with their balconies directly overhanging the sea—the whole crowned by a mosque.

Farther east still, on the southernmost point of Asia Minor, stood Anamourium, today a substantial village named Anamur. The city had a theatre and an odeum; on the shore stood a huge medieval fortress. The coast, especially towards the east, alternates between sheer cliffs jutting out into the sea and flat sandy beaches.

The inhabitants of Pamphylia and a part of Cilicia were pirates and slave-traders who terrorized the seas and, after each bold raid, withdrew with their booty to their unassailable hide-outs in the mountains. Shortly before Roman rule, the pirate clans of the entire Asia Minor coast had united to form a powerful state headed by dare-devil adventurers. To this day their eyries can be seen perched high above the gorges which intersect the plateau. With their enormous walls, towers, and parapets directly above the precipices they defied all attempts at subjugation.

In antiquity the dark cedar forests, which then covered the whole country, supplied the timber needed by the corsairs for their ships. The crenellated contours of the pirate fortresses high above the gorge cut through the mountains by the river Lamas look from the distance like magnificent fairy-tale cities—but they lie in ruins today and only bears and ibexes inhabit their massive walls.

The gates of Antioch mark the end of this coast of Asia Minor, a coast so abundant in natural beauty and in awe-inspiring reminders of a great and glorious past.

Cyprus

Island of Many Facets

Cyprus as seen on a map resembles a turtle with its head stretched out towards the east, as though anxious to reach the Asian mainland. Its shell is formed by the mountain range of Kyrenia in the north and the Troodos mountains in the west; the highest point of the latter, at 7000 feet, is called Mount Olympus—a name no doubt symbolical of the Greek character of the island. To the south, on the other hand, Cyprus opens out towards the not too distant regions of Africa. Small wonder that this strange island—to a far greater extent than any other Greek island or even the Greek mainland—has always been the cockpit of conflict between very diverse and invariably rival worlds, such as Hellenism and the East, Christianity and Islam, Rome and Byzantium, Greek and Turkish nationalism. With a length of 139 miles and a maximum width of 60 miles this third largest island in the Mediterranean—after Sicily and Sardinia—contains a positively confusing multitude and variety of architectural monuments of all periods and civilizations. Yet this historically saturated soil has by no means turned Cyprus into a kind of museum. On the contrary, the island is the home of a lively and at times hot-tempered people. To the tourist it moreover offers the fascinating contrast of inviting beaches, rugged mountains, harsh plains, and idyllic forests in a gently undulating landscape. Friends of nature and devotees of art alike will find much to delight them.

Legend

The origins of the island's population are shrouded in the mists of antiquity. All that can be proved is that Cyprus was settled by the Phoenicians at one time, and that the population, both in its way of life and its arts and crafts, was under marked Egyptian influence at a very early period. Following invasion by the armies of the Pharaoh

Thutmose III some time after 1500 B.C. the island came entirely under Egyptian rule. Between the fourteenth and eighth centuries B.C. the Greek Mycenaeans and Achaeans increasingly settled at this crossroads of world trade and eventually subdivided Cyprus into separate city states on the model of their native land.

Among the ancient Greeks this volcanic and probably somewhat harsh island was known as 'the happy island', and a great many legends were woven around it. Thus Aphrodite, the goddess of love, fertility, the sea and shipping, was supposed to have risen from the spume *(aphros)* of the sea, which had been fertilized by Uranus, near the city of Paphos on the western coast. Aphrodite, as witnessed by numerous remains of ancient temples and statues, was the object of extensive veneration. She was followed by the three Graces, whose veils, so Homer tells us, were dipped in the deliciously fragrant dew of Cypriot nights.

No one interested in life in Cyprus from the Stone Age to the Greco-Roman period should miss the magnificently stocked museum in Nicosia, which contains a particularly fine and well-preserved Aphrodite.

The island's present name is derived from the Phoenician word Koprus which described the cypress tree and was subsequently turned into the Greek word Kypros. The island's rich copper deposits became a legend even in antiquity, and our word copper thus goes back to Kypros and the earlier Koprus.

Byzantium and the National Church

For many centuries Cyprus led a contented and independent existence which scarcely differed from that of the Hellenistic world. But then, about 700 B.C., came the conquest of the island by the Assyrians, who were followed about 560 B.C. by the Egyptians. In 540 B.C. the Persians arrived, and under them the island was ruled by autocratic but humane kings. Alexander the Great reconquered Cyprus for Greece, but

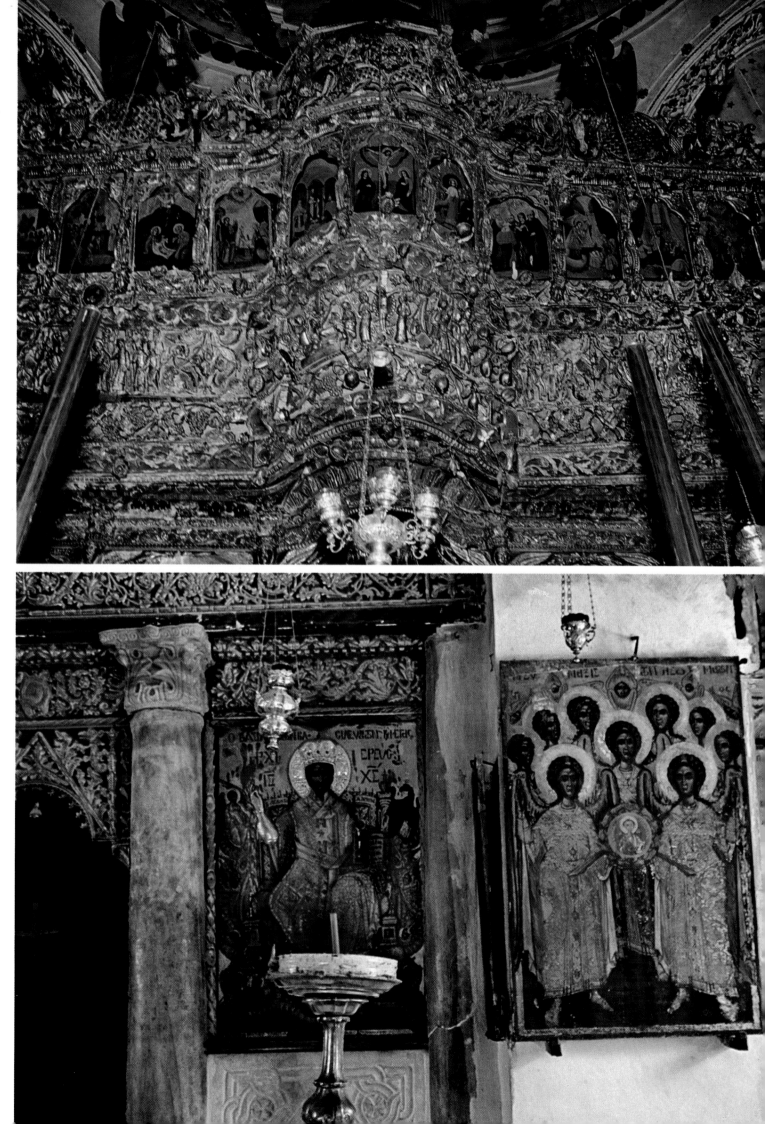

87
CHIOS
Iconostasis

88
CYPRUS
Early
Christian icons
at Lambusa

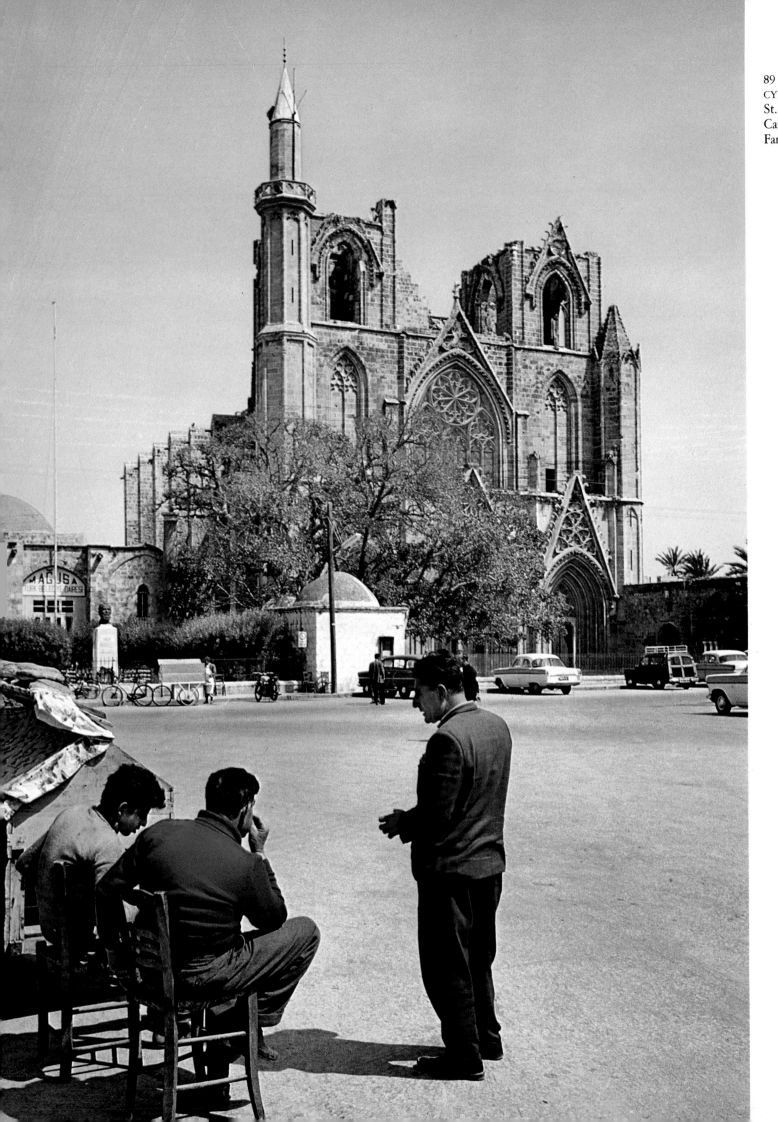

90 CYPRUS Byzantine church near Lambusa

91 CYPRUS Paphos, on the western coast

▷ 93
OFF CYPRUS
Rock of
Aphrodite

only a few centuries later the island was seized by the Egyptian Ptolemies. Nevertheless, through all the ups and downs of its history, the island preserved its Hellenistic character until the Romans took possession of it in 54 B.C. Under them the cities were given back their autonomy.

Rome's attempts to latinize the island remained unsuccessful. At a later date the Roman Catholic Church proved similarly incapable of making any headway against the vigorous resistance of Hellenism.

The first protagonists of Christianity in Cyprus were the Apostle Paul and Barnabas, who was later to be canonised and is now regarded as the real founder of the Cypriot Church. No visitor to the island should omit visiting the Monastery of St. Barnabas, situated near the ruins of Salamis in the east of the island. The monastery itself and the church belonging to it look impressive enough in the bare landscape, but they have been extensively restored and are not particularly beautiful. On the other hand, the visitor will find a small fountain with fresh water under magnificent eucalyptus trees—an ideal place for a rest. The monastery is inhabited by only a few novices in the charge of three senior brothers with long white beards; these monks devote their time exclusively to the painting of icons, but they receive all visitors with great charm and courtesy. The place is a refuge filled with the true peace of God, a peace that seems to belong to a bygone age. Yet one realizes here that St. Barnabas continued to influence the island's history well beyond the date of his death, and indeed may be said to be influencing it to this day.

From its very beginnings the Cypriot Church has exhibited a marked desire for self-government. This was the case even after the partition of the Roman Empire in A.D. 330, when Cyprus became part of the Greco-Christian empire of Byzantium. The Archbishop of Salamis in Cyprus immediately rejected all interference. He alone was to administer the ten bishoprics of the island. The Council of Ephesus in 431 eventually reconciled itself to this autonomy of the Cypriot Church—but not so the Patriarch of Antioch. He argued that, at the foundation of the Byzantine Empire,

Cyprus had been subordinate to the Prefecture of Antioch, and that Antioch was an apostolic foundation by St. Paul and had only subsequently brought the Gospel to Cyprus.

It was the Archbishop Anthemius of Constantia—as Salamis later called itself—who put a pious end to this continuous threat from Antioch. At just the right moment—in the year 477—the Archbishop had a vision in which St. Barnabas appeared to him and revealed to him the place where he was buried. And lo and behold: Anthemius found the Saint's tomb with his mortal remains; and, what was more, the Saint was found to be holding in his hands a gospel written by Matthew himself. Anthemius thereupon presented this precious manuscript to the Emperor Zeno of Byzantium who, out of gratitude for this princely gift, put it on record that Cyprus was an apostolic foundation and therefore entitled to ecclesiastical independence. Zeno subsequently granted to the Archbishop Anthemius all imperial privileges, such as the purple robe of the cardinal, the sceptre, and the red ink for his signature. Henceforward the existence of the Cypriot National Church was not to be challenged.

The consequences of this event fifteen centuries ago are still reflected in today's Cyprus conflict. It placed the island in a position when it could, to a very considerable extent, manage its own affairs in all future disputes, and act independently of Byzantium and later of Athens.

A word or two may be appropriate here about the strange position which the Greek clergy occupies in politics. Religion and nationalism form an inseparable union. The National Church, since it is not subject to Rome or any other superior outside power, is at the same time a religious community and a political organization. The religious leaders are the representatives of the Church just as they are those of the people and its *élite*. Above all, they have been the advocates and champions of Hellenism in times of peril and occupation. If, therefore, the fact that the present Archbishop of Cyprus, Makarios, also occupies the supreme office in the State offends our own Western sensibilities, we should remember that, from the point of view of a Greek Orthodox

Cypriot, this arrangement is not only entirely natural but must seem to him, in to-day's critical circumstances, essential.

But to return to St. Barnabas. Archbishop Anthemius had a chapel built next to the present church for the Apostle, and had him reburied there. At the same time he reserved the tomb alongside the saint for himself. Subsequently the two sarcophagi were found under the ruins of this chapel, broken open. They were empty and robbed of their relics. Only one fresco survives to illustrate for us the turbulent history of the monastery. Finally, the visitor should not forget to place his ear against a small hole in a column. This is said to prevent deafness.

The Princes of Lusignan

From 330 to 1191 Cyprus remained part of the Byzantine Empire. Hellenism developed vigorously, but a few sporadic incursions by Arab hordes from the Syrian coast resulted in the destruction of many a fine architectural monument from ancient antiquity or the early Christian period, and in the devastation of large tracts of land.

During the third Crusade Richard the Lionheart, King of England, took possession of the island and promptly sold it to the Knights Templar. The hostility of the Hellenistic population, however, caused the Order of the Templars nothing but difficulties and so, at the request of King Richard, they resold the island to Guy de Lusignan, the dethroned King of Jerusalem, a nobleman from the French city of Poitou, who paid for it 100,000 gold pieces.

The Princes of Lusignan, who ruled the island from 1192 until 1489, proved to be efficient governors, and trade and commerce flourished under them. They also showed considerable understanding of the Greek character of the population, but they were only able temporarily to delay the inevitable clash between the Greek and the Roman Churches. Needless to say, the Papacy was reluctant to forgo this favourable opportunity of incorporating Cyprus in the Latin sphere to which the House of Lusignan belonged. Thus, a Roman Catholic hierarchy established itself in Cyprus and succeeded in gradually reducing the number of Greek Orthodox bishops. As hostility flared up more openly, numerous Greek churches were looted and more and more new Roman churches built—the latter bearing the unmistakable stamp of the French Gothic style and therefore, to this day, somewhat foreign in the Cypriot setting, even though the architectural beauty and good taste of most of them is undisputed. When Pope Alexander IV issued his *Bulla Cypria* in 1260, which subordinated the island entirely to Rome, the embittered Greek Cypriots retreated into their monasteries in the interior of the island and turned these into veritable national and spiritual fortresses. The Lusignans, whose own impotence in the exacerbated clash between the eastern and western Churches was becoming increasingly obvious, did not oppose these developments.

To make up for their passivity in the conflict between the Churches, the Lusignan rulers engaged in campaigns of conquest in Asia Minor, where they occupied the Turkish province of Teke. Famagusta on the eastern coast of Cyprus became the hub of east-west trade and thus the most prosperous city in eastern Christendom. About the turn of the thirteenth and fourteenth centuries, however, the island became the scene of savage fighting. The Mamelukes sacked the cities of Larnaca and Limassol on the southern coast and inflicted a crushing defeat on the Cypriot army in 1425. Venice and Genoa were now competing for possession of the island, which was increasingly falling a prey to anarchy. King James II, the last king of the House of Lusignan, desperately married a rich Venetian lady of a most noble family in order to save his throne with the support of Venice. After his death, however, his widow had no alternative but to hand over the island to Venice.

Venetian Intermezzo

Venice accomplished the formal incorporation of the island in 1489. The Venetians endeavoured to extract all they could from Cyprus but, on the other hand, as a kind of collateral, they tried to protect the island against piratical raids from the nearby mainland. For that reason they developed the ramparts of Famagusta on the exposed east coast into a massive system of fortifications which is now a great tourist attraction. Nowadays one can take a peaceful stroll along them and enjoy the magnificent panorama.

Venice's rule became so oppressive that the Cypriots no longer shrank from the idea of casting out the devil through Beelzebub. They favoured the Turkish incursions and sometimes even hailed them as liberators.

Turkish Rule

At first it seemed that by supporting the Turks the islanders had done the right thing. Initially, the Turks—whose rule lasted from 1571 until 1878—treated the island with considerable generosity. They gave a large part of the ownerless land to the Greek Orthodox Church, they fully restored the independence of the Patriarchy and they granted the people freedom of religious practice. Their hostility was aimed solely against Latin Christianity, and in this attitude they enjoyed the enthusiastic support of the Greek Cypriots. The Turks looted the Roman Catholic churches and turned them into mosques—a circumstance which has left a strange stamp on several cities of the island.

Thus the Cathedral of St. Sophia, towering over the capital of Nicosia, is a Gothic building, but instead of the expected church towers it has two minarets. It is a rather odd piece of architecture, especially when seen against the Byzantine churches in its vicinity. 'Absurdly beautiful' is how an English writer described it. His description would be even more apt of the minaret which has been grafted upon the Gothic church of St. Nicholas in Famagusta.

Needless to say, some of the land abandoned by its former Venetian owners was taken over by Turkish soldiers and officials, and, as the island remained underpopulated, more Turks kept arriving from Anatolia to settle in Cyprus.

The marriage of convenience between Greeks and Turks did not last very long. The Turks proved to be poor administrators and rather too fond of a parasitical life. Drought, locusts, plague, and other epidemics further contributed to the utter decline of the once prosperous island. In fact, it became so impoverished and destitute that serious unrest broke out more than once among the population in the seventeenth and eighteenth centuries.

The Ottoman Empire itself soon became the Sick Man of Europe and was proving increasingly powerless in dealing even with its own officials in the countries it had annexed. In Cyprus things came to such a pass that Constantinople entered into an alliance with the island's Greek inhabitants against the insubordinate Turkish officials. The Sultan deprived the Turkish officials of the right to levy taxes—since they did not transfer the revenues to Turkey anyway—and handed this privilege over to the Church. Consequently the power of the Patriarchate increased to such an extent that disturbances broke out among the Turkish inhabitants of the island. Agreement was eventually reached on the lines that the Turkish Governor and the Archbishop would jointly run the government of the island. However, this idyllic arrangement did not last long. The Greek war of liberation against the Porte in the early nineteenth century was bound to have its repercussions in Cyprus. The struggle between the two sections of the population led to terrible bloodshed. Greek Cypriot freedom-fighters were beheaded in large numbers, and the island did not succeed then in casting off the Turkish yoke.

Britain's Key to the East

The year 1869 marked the opening of the Suez Canal, and the Mediterranean suddenly gained an enormous strategic importance. 'Cyprus is the key to Western Asia', the British Prime Minister Disraeli wrote to Queen Victoria, and in 1878 the British placed the island under their control. The Turkish Sultan, totally weakened by his disastrous war against Russia, was unable to put up any resistance, and contented himself with being recognized as the nominal sovereign of Cyprus. The Greek Cypriots gladly accepted the British presence, in the hope that one day London would grant them full independence, as well as granting it to the other islands off Asia Minor, whereupon they would be able to join up with Greece.

When Turkey sided with Britain's enemies in the First World War Britain promptly annexed Cyprus and offered the island to Greece if the King of the Hellenes would join the Allies. The King, however, hesitated for a whole two years, with the result that Britain later no longer considered herself bound by her earlier promise. The peace treaties of Sèvres (1920) and Lausanne (1923) finally confirmed British rule over the island.

The Greek Cypriot nationalists thereupon rallied in a movement which more and more vociferously demanded union (Enosis) with the Greek mother-country. Serious disturbances occurred, and the British decision to deport a large number of especially militant clergy merely added fuel to the flames. After the Second World War, when London granted independence to India, Pakistan, Ceylon, and then to one African possession after another, the Greek Cypriots' disinclination to collaborate with the British turned into boundless hatred of them. Colonel Grivas organized Eoka, a terrorist movement which henceforward set the general tone. All British ideas of a settlement and all attempted compromise proposals envisaging new constitutions were bound to founder in this political climate. The Turkish Cypriots, who represented only 17.5 per cent of the population, did not remain quiet either. They were afraid that, in the event of the island's union with Greece, the Greek majority would squeeze them out completely; they therefore demanded partition of the island and an exchange of populations between the two parts.

Archbishop Makarios, a militant opponent of British overlordship, was exiled to the Seychelles in 1956 and, though released the following year, was not allowed to return to Cyprus until 1959. He then came out in favour of independence for the island, whereas Grivas continued to champion Enosis. Thus a rift came about in the Cypriot liberation movement between its spiritual and military leaders. Makarios finally agreed to a compromise with London, especially as he regarded the proposed political arrangements as no more than an interim solution.

The 1959 Treaties

The new Cyprus Constitution, which was hammered out after protracted negotiations between the interested parties, is based on a rather complicated system of treaties worked out in Zürich and London in 1959. Turkey waived its demand to a partition of the island and Greece waived its claims to Enosis. London recognized the autonomy of the island and merely reserved for itself the right to maintain the British air and naval bases in Cyprus. On August 16th, 1960, Cyprus was proclaimed an independent republic and shortly afterwards was accepted into the United Nations. Cyprus moreover successfully applied for admission to the British Commonwealth. The treaties, which were to provide the basis for the future common government of the two parts of the population, contain the following main points:

(1) The President of the country shall be a Greek and the Vice-President a Turk. In matters of foreign policy and the island's security both the President and the Vice-President shall have an absolute right of veto.

(2) The Government shall consist of seven Greek and three Turkish ministers.

108

(3) The House of Representatives shall consist of thirty-five Greek and fifteen Turkish representatives. To pass into law a legislative proposal shall require the majority of both national groups among the representatives.

(4) The Turks shall be entitled to 30 per cent of all posts in the administration and in the police, as well as to 40 per cent in the Army.

Archbishop Makarios was elected President of the Republic and Dr. Kücük, a Turkish physician, was elected Vice-President.

It will be seen that this elaborately framed system of treaties grants the Greeks a position of primacy while at the same time embodying guarantees to prevent the mechanical outvoting of the Turkish minority. The Turks are able, either by the veto of their Vice-President or by a negative vote of their parliamentary group, to foil any decision of the Greek majority. Moreover, their share of administrative posts, at 30 to 40 per cent, is relatively high considering that the Turks account for less than 20 per cent of the population. Since the two national groups frequently hold violently divergent views on all kinds of everyday administrative issues, the result of these arrangements before long was that the Turks engaged in systematic obstruction and thus paralysed the entire administrative apparatus. Behind every Greek proposal they suspected, rightly or wrongly, a plot against their minority rights. In short, the political climate did not favour coexistence and the Constitution remained a dead letter.

Outbreak of the Conflict

The conflict came out into the open on 30th November 1963 when Makarios sent a letter to Kücük violently criticizing the Constitution and adding: 'It prevents Greeks and Turks from co-operating in a spirit of friendship and understanding, it compromises relations between them, and it increases discord rather than concord.' In his letter Makarios invited the Turks to waive their right of veto, which he said was paralysing the administration, as well as the practice of separate voting by national groups in the Assembly. He moreover demanded that the principle of separate Greek and Turkish administrations in the major towns should be scrapped and that the rule granting the Turks their large number of officials should be abolished.

Makarios's proposals in fact amounted to a suspension of the Constitution to which he himself had put his name. Naturally, the Turks angrily rejected these proposals. They regarded them as an attempt by the Archbishop to scrap all guarantees protecting the Turkish minority and to put it at the mercy of the Greek majority. Turkish demands for the partition of the island were again being voiced with redoubled determination and a positive proposal to this effect was tabled. This envisaged the granting of the north of the country, including Famagusta, to the Turks, with the town of Nicosia being divided. This plan involved the resettlement of some 50,000 Turks and 100,000 Greeks. The Greeks objected to this proposal for partition and resettlement by pointing out that it would give the Turks 40 per cent of the island's cultivated land against their present 15 per cent. The Turks would, moreover, gain possession of 100 industrial enterprises, whereas at present they owned a mere six. In the course of various attempts at mediation, in several of which the United Nations took a hand, it became clear that the Greeks were equally opposed to partition proposals more favourable to them because they simply wanted to avoid partition of the island at all costs.

Meanwhile the political fever kept rising in the island until savage incidents occurred between Greek and Turkish Cypriots, claiming a large number of casualties. Wherever the Turks lived in more or less compact communities they barricaded themselves —an arrangement which at least enabled the UN peace-keeping detachments to take up positions along the demarcation lines and thus to prevent major clashes.

A solution to the Cyprus problem has so far been made more difficult by the fact that Nicosia and Athens are not pursuing the same aims. Athens, no matter who is in power there, continues to call for Enosis. Makarios, on the other hand, while not opposing Enosis, wants to use it as a bartering counter rather than accept it unconditionally. In his view Cyprus must first gain complete independence and then open negotiations with Athens. He is clearly intent on ensuring some kind of autonomy for the island and on preserving the autocephalous position of the Cypriot National Church, whose Patriarch he is, even after union with Greece. Another consideration is the fact that Cyprus depends very largely on exports of exactly the same agricultural produce as Greece. As a Commonwealth country it now enjoys valuable preferential tariffs which it would lose after union with Greece. For that reason the Greek Cypriot business community believes that the question of the island's exports must first be settled. Only when firm contractual obligations have been entered into by the Greek Government could Enosis be brought about.

Athens distrusts Nicosia and fears that it may intend to torpedo Enosis at the last moment. Nicosia, on the other hand, suspects Athens of wanting direct negotiations with Ankara with a view to facing the Cypriots with a *fait accompli,* without consulting them beforehand. This mistrust is reflected also in the fact that Athens appointed Grivas—promoted to the rank of General—commander of the Greek contingent in Cyprus while Makarios repeatedly demanded his recall.

Greeks and Turks

The Turkish minority, estimated—according to which side has prepared the statistics —at 16 to 20 per cent of the population, is scattered about all six districts of the island. It is somewhat more numerous in the towns than in the countryside. It is most in evidence in the district of Paphos, with over 22 per cent, and least in the district of Kyrenia, with less than 13 per cent. Of the villages, 323 have a mixed population, 246 are exclusively Greek, and 56 are entirely Turkish.

It is occasionally claimed that the Greek Cypriots are not really Greek. It is true, of course, as a supporter of this view has recently written, that few countries in the world have attracted so many different nations and civilizations as the island of Cyprus, situated as it was at the crossroads of so many trade routes between east and west, and north and south, in the ancient world. Indeed, it was not only Greeks who inhabited the island but also Assyrians, Egyptians, Romans, Crusaders of various origins, French, Genoese, Venetians, Turks, and British. Certainly the cultural influence of these conqueror nations must not be underrated, but much the same could be said about the Greek mainland where the Greeks of today are likewise no longer identical with the Hellenes of antiquity. It would be a mistake to put the foreign racial element too high. Of course there have been mixed marriages. But they have been very much the exception. The foreign rulers usually kept a very strict social barrier between themselves and their subjects, and the enslaved Greeks' hatred of all foreigners acted as a solid barrier against race mixture. Greek women who allowed themselves to be enticed into the Turkish harems were expelled from the Greek community and absorbed by the Turks. Greek men very rarely married Turkish girls, or if they did so they joined the Islamic faith and thereby became Turks. It could therefore be claimed with far greater justification that the Turkish blood in the island is less pure than the Greek, especially since the Turkish conquerors were very largely janissaries press-ganged from among subject nations and forcibly converted to Islam. And a great number of janissaries were undoubtedly of Greek origin.

What matters is the fact that the Greek Cypriots have never ceased to speak the same language as their Greek brethren on the other islands and on the mainland, that they observe the same faith, that they celebrate the same festivals and that, apart from insignificant local divergencies, their way of life in no way differs from that of the rest of the Greeks. For that reason there would be no point in describing the national character or way of life of the Greek Cypriots in any detail since this would merely be a repetition of what has been said in this book elsewhere.

The only peculiar feature of Cyprus, in fact, is its considerable Turkish minority which refuses at all costs to integrate with the Greek community and which isolates itself from the Greeks wherever possible. A few remarks about these Turkish Cypriots would not therefore be out of place.

The numerous Muslim incursions which Cyprus had to suffer in the course of its turbulent history have left no Turkish traces in the island whatever. The origin of the present-day Turkish community therefore goes back only to the island's conquest in 1571. Presumably the Turkish troops which took part in the occupation of the island themselves expressed the wish to settle there. They were presently joined by the many officials whom the Sultan had to send across to look after the island's administration, and finally by a great many traders—although most of these stayed in the island only temporarily.

Within a year of the conquest, the Turkish community is said to have numbered about 30,000. This total was soon augmented by 5000 families from Anatolia—mainly peasants and artisans whose emigration was encouraged by the Sultan. Naturally, no accurate statistics are available from that period. Nevertheless it seems that by about 1750 the Greek and Turkish inhabitants of the island were about evenly balanced. In 1878, when the British occupied the island, the Turks were clearly in the majority. After that came a sudden decline. The first accurate figures, dating from 1888, record only 45,000 Turks to 137,000 Greeks. At present the ratio is 115,000 to 450,000. One would therefore be justified in saying that the British annexation of the island has saved its original Greek character. This impression is strengthened if one looks at the motives of the Turkish re-emigration into the old country. These may be summed up as follows.

Until the British annexation the Turkish Cypriots kept their Turkish citizenship. The British, however, offered them the alternatives of either becoming British subjects or else returning to Turkey. This explains, in part at least, the sudden start of a massive re-emigration. The emigrants settled chiefly in Adana and Mersin on the Turkish coast, which have a similar climate to Cyprus and which are to this day inhabited by former Cypriot Turks.

The Turkish Cypriots have always been inferior to the Greek Cypriots in education and in vocational skills. While Turkish rule lasted this disadvantage was largely offset by certain privileges which they enjoyed *vis-à-vis* the subjected Greeks. With the loss of these privileges under the British they were no longer in a position to compete with the Greeks and therefore frequently preferred to return to their old country. Even nowadays we find few Turks in senior positions in the island. Most of them are simple peasants and artisans, only very occasionally are they big merchants or businessmen. Their middle-class has always produced a strikingly large number of men for the Cyprus civil service. The Greeks have not begrudged them these posts, which in terms of financial reward are not very attractive. For that reason also they readily granted them the disproportionately high percentage of civil service posts in 1959, especially as this allowed them to develop their own dominant position in the island's economy.

The numerically less important Turkish *élite* found itself at a disadvantage under the British. There were no higher schools to provide a Turkish education for their children and there was not a single university for them. Their return to Turkey, therefore, had a markedly detrimental effect on the intellectual life of the remaining Turks. Between the two world wars the shortage of men made itself felt among the Turkish Cypriots in a highly undesirable way. The women were only too ready to enter into unions with Syrians and Jordanians who enjoyed the services of a special 'agency' for that purpose in Larnaca.

It is a curious fact that even under British rule the Turkish Cypriots refused to give up their 'apartheid'. In all their actions they closely followed the line taken by Turkey, just as if Cyprus were still a part of Turkey. Thus the Turkish Cypriots faithfully echoed all the changes wrought by the Turkish national revolution under Atatürk, and to this day they closely follow the official line pursued by whatever Government is in power in Ankara. Vice-President Kücük never pursued a line of his own. In contrast to Makarios, who is never too anxious to consult the Greek Government, Kücük would never dream of acting independently. He receives all his instructions from Ankara and does not aspire to being more than a simple executive official of the Turkish Government.

In dealing with foreign tourists the Turkish Cypriots act with exquisite oriental courtesy. Such tourists, incidentally, encounter no difficulties on the part of the UN peacekeeping forces when wishing to cross the demarcation lines, provided they show their passports. The Turks proudly show off their mosques and museums, but they observe their festivals in strict isolation from the non-Islamic world. The only impression a visitor will gain of the Turkish 'reservations' is that life there is on a rather primitive level.

The Economy

Cyprus is essentially an agricultural island and has remained largely unaffected by the prosperity of industrial countries. In spite of the pull of the towns, over 40 per cent of the population continues to cultivate the land, where numerous flocks of sheep lend an idyllic touch to the stony harshness of the landscape. Some 47 per cent of the soil is not fit for cultivation. A further 18 per cent is covered by forests and 10 per cent is pasture. This means that a mere 18 per cent of the total area is left for cultivation, allowing for the area taken up by towns, rivers, and roads. Finding adequate employment for the rapidly increasing population will continue to be a major problem. Unemployment fluctuates between 4000 and 7000 but this does not include the underemployed in the countryside whose number cannot be statistically determined. Mechanization of agriculture makes it increasingly difficult to create new employment on the land.

These difficulties are offset, up to a point, by the island's mineral wealth—principally the mining of copper, iron, and chromium. Total exports in 1965 consisted of 56.5 per cent in agricultural produce and 38.5 per cent of minerals.

Another promising aspect is the growing production and export of citrus fruit (oranges, lemons, and grapefruit), of grapes, wine, and, to a lesser extent, potatoes. These categories account for 75 per cent of all agricultural exports. The Government hopes that, by means of up-to-date agricultural machinery and improved irrigation facilities, the production of citrus fruit, which is in great demand, can be increased by 40 to 50 per cent over the next few years. The principal consumer is the British market, but if Cyprus were to unite with Greece, and consequently lose the advantages of imperial preference, this market could easily be lost.

The fresh grapes exported by Cyprus are also of excellent quality. Production of these rose to 125,000 tons in 1965. The island has also been successful in increasing its export of wine from 2.7 million gallons in 1959 to nearly 3 million gallons in 1965—but this has been entirely due to British help.

The Cinderella of the island is grain-cultivation. Cyprus is still obliged to import some 20,000 tons of grain annually—between a third and a half of its domestic requirements.

Meat, milk, eggs, and honey account for 26 per cent of the total agricultural revenue. Cattle-rearing is difficult because of the island's dry climate. There is a lack of good pasturage for cattle, and thus goats and sheep continue to be the only livestock of any importance.

The sea which washes the island's coasts is disappointingly poor in fish. The Cypriot fishing industry employs only just over a thousand people who have to work very hard for an extremely meagre reward. The fishing fleet numbers a mere 300 rowing and sailing boats, 180 motor-boats, and 10 sloops.

All the major towns, with the exception of Nicosia, the capital, are on the coast. They are, in descending order of importance, Famagusta, Limassol, and Larnaca. Yet only the port of Famagusta is able to accommodate ships of 420 feet in length and a draught of 23 feet. Its turnover is about 40,000 tons of merchandise per month.

Since the proclamation of the island's independence in 1960 the Government has placed great hopes in tourism in order to balance its trade deficit. There has been no lack of effort to increase the flow of holiday visitors: modernization of the airport of Nicosia, widening and improvement of the island's principal roads, the new monumental Hilton hotel in Nicosia, and the attractive yacht harbour that is being developed at Famagusta. International motor-boat races, ballet weeks, wine festivals, and a variety of other events designed to attract an exacting crowd of foreign tourists are being increasingly promoted in the 'happy island'. The only obstacle at the moment is the political unrest. It is often difficult, even on the strength of personal experience, to convince a foreigner that he will scarcely be aware of these matters and that he will be able to move in complete safety, both among Greeks and Turks, wherever he chooses to go in Cyprus.